GOD AND EVIL

GOD AND EVIL

In the Theology of St Thomas Aquinas

HERBERT McCABE OP

Edited and Introduced by
Brian Davies OP

continuum

Published by the Continuum International Publishing Group

The Tower Building   80 Maiden Lane
11 York Road   Suite 704
London   New York
SE1 7NX   NY 10038

www.continuumbooks.com

First published 2010

British Library Cataloguing-in-Publication Data
A catalogue record for this book is available from the British Library.

ISBN 978-0826–41304-8

Designed and typeset by Free Range Book Design & Production Ltd
Printed and bound by the MPG Books Group

CONTENTS

FOREWORD

Terry Eagleton

Those who were fortunate enough to know Herbert McCabe personally were aware that he had, at a highly conservative estimate, two sides to his personality. There was Herbert the razor-sharp logician who would pursue an argument with relentless precision and persistence; and there was Herbert the creative artist, with his flights of imaginative wit and edgy, perverse, Chestertonian delight in paradox. In some ways, the first persona acted as a defence against the passionate excesses of the second. It is the former McCabe, as Brian Davies notes in his Introduction, who holds sway in this wonderfully lucid, bracingly ambitious essay on evil; but the latter, later writer runs as a subdued subcurrent through the work, as though Thomas Aquinas were to have handed Herbert a clutch of his ideas with the injunction 'Here, make this stuff sound a bit more lively.' There are continuities as well as differences, then, between early and late McCabe. One such continuity is the first unveiling here of a character called Fred, who was to make frequent guest appearances in the later oeuvre.

Some of the paradoxes and *aperçus* in the book belong to Aquinas himself, while others are the work of his faithful interpreter. We learn, for example, that it is proper in Aquinas's view to say 'The human being exists' but not 'The Englishman exists,' a claim that will no doubt be greeted with acclaim in a good many outposts of the post-colonial world. We are informed that one dog can be more doggy than another, a proposition the English, if they existed, would surely be eager to endorse. God is not a moral being, and there is nothing that is natural or unnatural for him to do. Before he does something he has no reason for doing it rather than not doing it; rather, he *is* the reason for what he does. For St Thomas, so Herbert writes, 'to have a concept of goodness in the sense in which we have a concept of redness would be to comprehend God'. As for evil, the other term in the book's title, Herbert argues that there cannot be anything evil which is not also in some respect good, since evil belongs to created things, and creation is good in itself. It does not make sense to say that the essence of anything as such is evil. It is good in itself that there are lentils and equilateral triangles around the place. This, of course, also commits us to the unpalatable proposition that it is a good thing that Britney Spears exists, or that Michael Jackson once did; but however palpably absurd the claim might appear, we simply have to cling to faith here against all the seductions of reason.

A stone, Aquinas tells us, is more perfect the nearer to the centre of the earth it gets; and this is the cue in this book for a surreally Beckettian disquisition on the difference between stones and rats. We are also told that God accounts for causes being causes and purposes being purposes. Creation is that kind of causing which is no particular kind of causing – one which makes all the difference without making a difference at all. It is not possible to create well or badly, Herbert points out, in the sense that it is possible to do something well or badly. The opposite of creation is nothing; but since we cannot conceive of nothing, we cannot conceive of creation either. Some philosophers regard it as conceivable that the world emerged from nothing, while others respond that this is impossible. Thomists, by contrast, argue that it is inconceivable that the world came from nothing, but that it did.

As a devout disciple of Aquinas, Herbert McCabe was of course an essentialist – a doctrine that for postmodernism is only mildly less reprehensible than paedophilia. In postmodern eyes, essences restrict the free play of the world, freezing its incorrigible plurality into a sort of Platonic stasis. It is striking, then, that this book, following Aquinas, sees essences and plurality as intimately related. The essence of something, which simply means what kind of thing it is, tells us what kind of language is appropriate in speaking of it; and given that there are many kinds of things, there are enough sorts of languages in the world to delight the heart of the most pluralistic of postmodernists. There is no general way of talking about the world. On this the Thomist and the postmodernist are at one. There are just specific idioms. If we don't ask what things are, we are in danger of confusing one language-game with another; and this, Herbert considers, is where the problem of evil arises. It is more a problem about our language than a problem about God. 'The problem of evil is not a question about what we are prepared to allow God to do. It is a question about what our language will allow us to say.'

Language was one of Herbert's great passions from start to finish, so it is interesting to see it playing such a vital role in his theology as early as this essay. The early Wittgenstein wanted to enforce a strict distinction between what could and what could not be said; but though Herbert was a dedicated Wittgensteinian all his life, he was aware that there were forms of discourse which transgressed or deconstructed this distinction by trying to articulate truths which they acknowledged to be finally beyond speech. If literary language was one of these, theology – that persistently failing metaphor – was another.

Aquinas's notion of analogy, Herbert comments, is concerned with the failure of words to behave in the ways that might be expected of them. Perhaps the book overstates its case a little when it seems to claim that the problem of evil arises *only* because of confusing the language proper to God with the language proper to some enormously powerful thing. The transcendence of God means that he is beyond the world and the language in which the problem of evil can be stated; and this, for the book, is the key to the whole affair. Such language is forced to employ words outside their proper context, asking questions of God which can only intelligibly be asked about creatures. But this is not simply to throw in the philosophical towel and deny that anything useful can be said. Witness the existence of this richly argumentative book.

Does the book, then, solve the theological problem of evil? Of course not. 'God', Herbert writes, 'is not an explanation of the world,' and no statement about the former entails any statement about the latter. So we are back to the ending of the Book of Job. In those final enigmatic verses, God does not explain to his afflicted servant why he has so callously tormented him. As far as that goes, he tells him, more or less, to get lost. Instead, he turns the questioning on Job himself, though the form of the questions is rhetorical: 'Where were you when I laid the foundations of the earth? ... Have you entered into the springs of the sea, or walked in the recesses of the deep?' Yahweh is not to be understood here as pulling rank. There is no macho comparison of muscle-size at stake. He is simply reminding Job that he is, after all, God, and thus by definition beyond the imputed meanings and purposes of human beings. How on earth could he be God and not be? What would be the point of a completely intelligible God?

So the book does not resolve the problem of evil. Instead, it radically recontextualises it, in a way that clarifies rather than dispels its mystery. Having reached the final page of Herbert's volume, we now know rather better how to talk about what we can't talk about. If all authentic theology holds saying and the unsayable in perpetual tension, there could be no finer example of it than a work which acknowledges mystery in the most rigorously exact of terms.

INTRODUCTION

Herbert McCabe OP died in 2001. During his lifetime he published four books and many articles. At the time of his death he was widely recognised as one of the most gifted English-speaking theologians and philosophers of his generation. For many years he was editor of the journal *New Blackfriars*, to which he contributed numerous and vigorous editorials. He lectured at Oxford University and at universities in the USA and elsewhere. He preached on a regular basis (as befitted his status as a Dominican friar, which is what he was first and foremost). He was an indefatigable exponent of and commentator on the thought of St Thomas Aquinas (c. 1225–1274). He also did a number of radio and television broadcasts.

Herbert made me his literary executor, and I am now privileged to have edited five volumes based on material that he left behind at the time of his death. All of these volumes have received extremely good reviews, which is what I always expected them to do. The volumes in question are: *God Still Matters* (London and New York: Continuum, 2002), *God, Christ and Us* (London and New York: Continuum, 2003), *The Good Life* (London and New York: Continuum, 2005), *Faith Within Reason* (London and New York: Continuum, 2007), and *On Aquinas* (London and New York: Continuum, 2008). I was not surprised that these books were well received because of what I take to be Herbert's genius. He asked hard questions of key significance to both philosophers and theologians. And he always offered clear, well argued, and direct answers to them. Not too many people manage to pull off that trick.

But this sixth posthumously published volume is different from those just mentioned. While they were compiled from typescripts written by Herbert from around 1970 onwards, this book derives from what he wrote in 1957 at the age of thirty. It represents what we might call his early rather than his later period of writing. Herbert entered the Order of Preachers (the Dominicans) in 1949. Before completing his formal studies within the Order (and well before he became known to the reading public), he was directed to obtain a Licence in Sacred Theology (STL), a Dominican degree which requires candidates to prepare a written thesis to be defended before a committee of examiners. Candidates for the STL are also called upon to prepare a list of propositions, or 'theses', to be orally defended before the same committee. Herbert was examined for the STL on 26 June 1957. The title of his written thesis was *God and Evil in the Theology of St Thomas Aquinas*. This book is an edited version of that thesis.[1] The influence of Aquinas on

---

[1]   In editing the thesis I have done the following: (1) I translated Latin words and sentences which Herbert originally left untranslated; (2) I corrected some of Herbert's references to texts of Aquinas (some of them were not accurate), and I corrected some of his quotations of Latin texts written by Aquinas (some of these contained errors); (3) I changed Herbert's text so as to provide gender-inclusive language

Herbert can be seen in almost everything he went on to write. And ideas which he later frequently emphasised are much in evidence in his STL thesis.

I originally had reservations about trying to see this text through to publication. First, Herbert's thesis was never intended for a general readership (unlike most of the other things that he went on to write). The audience envisaged by its author was an examining committee consisting entirely of Dominicans.[2] And the work itself is clearly an academic dissertation, one which often makes assumptions that other kinds of essay would not.[3] Second, Herbert himself never took any steps to revise his thesis for publication. He went on to write some essays on God and evil, ones in which Aquinas features prominently. But he left his

---

and to avoid usage of the royal plural (as befitted an ecclesiastical dissertation written in the 1950s, Herbert's thesis talked constantly about 'man', 'men', and what 'we' have shown or are about to show); (4) I made a number of punctuation changes to Herbert's text so that it might read more smoothly to contemporary readers. Otherwise, though, I left the text alone. Readers should be assured that what they have in the present volume does not omit anything that Herbert had to say in his thesis when it comes to content.

[2] Fr Richard Finn OP, the current Regent of Studies of the English Dominican Province, tells me that Herbert's examiners included Ambrose Farrell OP, Ivo Thomas OP, Bonaventure Perquin OP, and Gervase Matthew OP.

[3] As readers of his published works will know very well, Herbert came to develop a highly engaging and personal style of writing, one displaying a characteristic 'voice', which is very accessible even to readers lacking any background on the matters with which he was concerned. By contrast, his STL thesis is a fairly formal work. Much that Herbert wrote could be described as 'chatty'. His STL thesis is not that.

STL thesis alone.[4] This made me wonder to what extent Herbert himself was happy about it as time passed. Yet I have always thought that the work contained some very good arguments and some extremely helpful accounts of Aquinas's thinking on a number of important and difficult issues. With the encouragement of Continuum, therefore, I have been happy to do my best to present it to contemporary readers.

In the light of much that has been written in recent years on the topic of God and evil, Herbert's text now reads as strikingly original. Contemporary discussions of God and evil seem largely dominated by attempts to show that God is or is not morally justified for permitting the evils we encounter (whether evils over which we have no control or those perpetrated by us). Herbert's approach is completely different. He seeks to ask what we might mean by 'good', 'evil', and 'God', and his focus is on what we might call 'the metaphysics of creation'. What can be thought of as existing, and in what sense of 'exists'? What can be thought of as caused by God? In what sense can we think of God as a cause? To what extent do we know what God is? And to what extent should our thinking about human causes be used when trying to talk about God as Creator? These are Herbert's main questions, and his treatment of them results in an approach to the topic of God and evil which is none too

---

[4] For an essay on God and evil published by Herbert in his lifetime, see chapter 3 of *God Matters* (London: Cassell, 1987). See also chapters 6 and 8 of *Faith Within Reason*. These chapters were not published by Herbert himself, but I know that he wanted the second of them to appear in print.

common these days. In this sense, the present work is indeed original.

In another sense it is not original at all, for Herbert is basically presenting and defending what Aquinas says about God and evil. The moral, perhaps, is that originality is in the eye of the beholder. To someone unfamiliar with Aquinas (and with the Aristotelian notions that inform much of his thinking), Aquinas and Herbert on evil will seem like something new. People with some serious grasp of the history of theology and philosophy will have a different perspective. So, perhaps, readers of this volume who are not already versed in the ideas of Aquinas are in for something of an 'eye opener'. What they shall certainly find is a clear and accurate account of some very fundamental aspects of Aquinas's thinking. They shall also find some valuable comments on them. Readers of this volume who already know something about Aquinas shall find it to be as illuminating on the exegetical front as anything that Herbert ever wrote about his favourite author.

One problem with the text (and this is another reason why I was initially hesitant about offering it for publication) is that in it exposition of Aquinas and evaluation of him are sometimes blurred in a way that was never the case in what Herbert later came to write. He nearly always made it clear what Aquinas actually said and where he did and did not agree with him. His STL thesis, however, sometimes provides accounts of Aquinas's teachings without holding them out at arm's length as matters to be defended or attacked. Though the thesis has plenty to say about the worth of Aquinas's thinking, it sometimes seems to treat

Aquinas as an authority in a way that Herbert did not in his subsequent writings. I have no doubt that it did so because the work was, as I have explained, something to be examined by a panel of Dominicans. Readers of what follows might care to bear this in mind and to be indulgent accordingly.

Herbert wrote a splendid paper called 'Categories' (originally published in *Dominican Studies*). I am presenting this paper as an Appendix to this volume since it deals with matters discussed in Herbert's STL thesis and will, I hope, help readers better to understand what he says there. I have also compiled a short bibliography of recently published texts with a bearing on what Herbert has to say in his thesis about Aquinas and God and evil. I do not know whether Herbert would have approved of this Bibliography. I offer it simply as an aid to people who might want to think further about the issues discussed by him.

In preparing what follows I have been much helped by my friend and colleague Michael Baur. He made me appreciate the extent to which Herbert's STL thesis might be illuminating to contemporary readers. I am also very grateful to Christopher Upham (who turned Herbert's thesis into an electronic text for me to work on) and to Turner Nevitt (who did a truly magnificent job of proof reading).

Brian Davies
Fordham University
New York

ONE

The Statement of the Problem

Arguments to show that there is no problem of evil and reasons to show that these arguments are invalid

The problem of evil can be stated as follows: Quite frequently horrible things happen. We know that we ought to do all in our power to prevent these things, but often we have not the means of doing so. If people had the means of preventing these things but did not do so, we should say that they were wicked. Sometimes, as we watch helplessly some suffering or iniquity, we say that there is nothing we can do and that nothing short of a miracle could save the situation. So, why does God not intervene? Good people do not intervene because they are powerless. Wicked people do not intervene because they are evil. Which of these groups does God resemble?

Against this analysis it may be argued that there is all the difference in the world between committing an evil and tolerating an evil. It is the former in virtue of which we say that someone is bad, but to tolerate an evil is not always the way of a wicked person. For example, if I allow someone innocent to be killed rather than tell a lie which would save that person, I am not committing an evil and I am in no sense guilty of the person's death or of anything else. It may be thought that when God permits an evil to occur he acts just like such a human being. How can we know, it may be asked, that God is able to prevent this evil without committing another evil?

In replying to this argument I should agree that someone who can only prevent an evil by committing another evil lacks the means of preventing the first one; such a person is indeed not wicked for tolerating the evil. Nevertheless, to be in a position in which one can only prevent an evil by committing another is to be of limited power, for it is always possible to imagine another way of preventing the evil, which a more powerful being could use. It is always possible to imagine that a miracle might occur. If we are to excuse God's inactivity on these grounds, we are admitting that his power is limited.

Again, it may be argued that to be unable to do what is impossible is not a mark of limited power. Thus an infinitely wise and powerful being would be unable to mention a prime number greater than 13 and less than 17. Now it is not possible to create a world that does not contain evil occurrences or evil things, and hence to say that God could only create a world containing evil is not to imply that his power is limited. That it is impossible to create a world that does not contain evil might be argued as follows: Evil is the opposite of good. Where there is evil there is not good, and where there is not evil there is good. Hence it is evil that formally sets a limit to good. To say that there is not evil is to say that good is unlimited. Now if the world were such that it contained no evil it would be unlimitedly or infinitely good and would thus be in no way different from God. But just as it is impossible for God to create himself, so it is impossible for him to create something in no way different from himself. Hence what he creates has to be less than infinitely good. Its goodness must be limited by some evil.

In replying to this argument I should agree that the words 'possible' and 'impossible' are used in two ways.

Sometimes we are speaking of what can occur, and sometimes we are speaking of what can be said. It is in the latter sense that we say that an infinitely powerful being cannot do what is impossible. Thus, when we say that such a being could not make a round square, we mean that the phrase 'round square' is not a name and hence cannot be the name of anything made by any being. God cannot make a round square just as he cannot make a hardly ever. It is sometimes said that the phrase 'created world containing no evil' is not a name because to be created, to be other than God, is the same as to contain evil. The notion that evil and good cannot be defined without reference to God is one that shall be shown to be fallacious in the course of this book; for the moment, however, it will suffice to point out a mistake in the argument just mentioned. Thus: It is necessary to distinguish two ways in which things are said to be opposites. Things are *contrary opposites* when the presence of one *implies* the absence of the other but the absence of one does not itself imply the presence of the other (as is case with, for example, black and white). They are *contradictory opposites* when the absence of one is *equivalent to* the presence of the other, and vice versa (as is the case with hot and cold). It is true that good and evil are opposites in the former sense, but not in the latter sense. Thus, the absence of good does not imply the presence of its contrary, evil. If there were no kangaroos there would be no good kangaroos. But it does not follow that there would be some evil kangaroos. So, although evil does limit good, it is not definable as the limit of good, and, in consequence, the argument just noted fails.

The above statement of the problem of evil asserted that, since there is evil in the world, God is either evil or of limited power. The two preceding arguments have sought and failed to show that either of these consequences need follow. But let us now consider arguments that claim that the dilemma fails because there is no evil in the world. This conclusion may be argued for in three ways.

In the first place it may be said that the assertion 'This is evil,' although an indicative sentence, has little in common with such sentences as 'This is red.' In particular, it may be said that while 'This is red' implies that there is redness in the world, it is not the case that 'This is evil' implies that there is evil in the world. The reason that might be given for this conclusion is that 'This is evil' is not a descriptive account of the thing referred to but, rather, an expression of disapproval of the thing combined with certain recommendations concerning it. Thus, it could be maintained that 'This orange is bad' is more like 'I dislike this orange,' or 'Don't eat this orange,' than it is like 'This orange is round.' Clearly to say 'I dislike this orange' or 'Don't eat this orange' is not to characterise the orange in any way. It is not to attribute anything to it or to describe it. In the same way, it may be claimed that when I say 'This orange is bad' I do not characterise, attribute anything to, or describe the orange.

A second argument might run as follows: It is true that 'This is evil' does assert the presence of evil in the world, but this assertion is false or at least it can never be known to be true. If we look at a few square inches of a painting, the design may seem to us ill-proportioned and the colours inharmonious, and we may be inclined to say that the painting is ugly. But when we see the whole painting and realise that what we formerly saw was only a part of the whole, we view the composition and colour in its proper context and it no longer looks ugly. In the same way, our knowledge of creation is confined to a few centuries of history and a few thousand miles of space. Is it not possible that what appears to us to be evil may, when seen in its proper context, appear as good? At any rate we cannot know that this will not be so, and the existence of a good God suggests that it will be so. An influential variant of this argument claims that evils suffered in this life will be counterbalanced by the joys of a life to come, so that when our existence is seen as a whole, it is seen to be good and not evil.

A third line of argument runs as follows: Evil is nothing real, it is simply the absence of good. Hence when we say that there is evil in the world, we cannot be asserting that there is something in the world. Evil is a mere negation that we sometimes mistakenly regard as a reality and hence problems about its origin and cause are out of place.

In reply to the first of these arguments I should argue that, while it is quite true that the assertion 'This is evil' is not the same type of statement as 'This is red' in that it does not attribute to the thing referred to a quality called 'evil', whereas the latter does attribute the quality of redness, nevertheless the assertion 'This is evil' need not, for that reason, be assimilated to expressions of approval or disapproval or to recommendations. The possibility of genuine statements that are not descriptive statements of the same kind as 'This is red' will be established below.

In reply to the second argument I would say that the phrase 'a part of the whole' can mean two things. Sometimes we take the world 'part' *formally*, to mean what cannot be considered apart from that of which it is a part. In this sense the back of a bus is a part of the bus. Sometimes, however, we use the world 'part' *materially* – to mean something that is a part of a whole but that can also be considered as a whole on its own. In this sense the wheels of a bus are parts of the bus. Now an arbitrarily chosen segment of a painting may be considered either as a painting on its own or as simply contributing to the painting of which it is a segment. In the former case it is a part materially, in the latter case, a part formally. In the latter case, when we see the picture as a whole we no longer consider the segment as an individual whole and hence we cease to speak of it at all. It is for this reason that we do not say that it is ugly or beautiful. But in the former case we may still say that the segment of the picture taken as an individual whole is ugly, even while admitting that the picture as a whole is beautiful. Now the events and things of this world are individual wholes (indeed they are the only individual wholes that we know), and if they are parts of the whole universe they are parts materially. Hence we may still say that some of them are evil even while admitting that the universe as a whole is good. But the problem of evil as characterized above is set for us not by a (hypothetically) good whole universe but by those evil parts of the universe that we know. It might be said in reply to this point that what appear to us as individual things are not really individual things but formal parts of the universe. To this I reply that if we cannot use the words 'thing', 'evil' and 'good' about what appear to us to be evil or good things, then there is nothing about which we can use them. How did we ever learn to use such words? It is understandable that we should be wrong occasionally, but it is not possible that we should always be wrong.

In reply to the third argument I should say that it depends on the error already exposed of confusing contrary and contradictory opposites. Contradictory opposites have nothing in common. So, if one is real, the other is not. But contrary opposites share a common subject or field of reference, and both are real in so far as this subject or field of reference is real. This point will be further developed later in this essay.

Finally, it may be argued that granting that there is evil in the world, and granting that the responsible cause must be either evil or weak, there does not arise a problem about God since the cause in question is not God but human beings. It may be said that, although to attribute the evil in the world to any other created cause would not be to absolve God of responsibility, since all other created causes are determined in their action by God, nevertheless, to attribute it to human beings is to absolve God from responsibility, since the action of people is free and not determined by God. God can no more be counted guilty of our misdeeds than a father can be accounted guilty of his son's misdeeds.

In replying to this line of thought I should agree that God is not morally responsible for our misdeeds; such responsibility belongs entirely to us. The reason for this, however, is not that our freedom makes us independent of God in the way in which a son is independent of his father. This can be proved in two ways. In the first place to be created is to depend upon the creator absolutely and without qualification. Other causes bring about this or that in a thing, but creation brings about everything in the thing. It follows that 'a created thing independent of its creator' is a self-cancelling expression and not a possible name of anything. In the second place to say that a human being is free is not to say that he or she is independent of God, and to say that other creatures are not free is not to say that they are dependent on God. In determining whether something is free or not (whether, for example, a man is acting freely or under compulsion, whether external or internal) no reference is made to God. Someone who does not know that God exists can make this judgement as well as someone who does. It follows that to be free does not mean to be independent of God.

The previous six arguments have sought to show that the problem of evil as stated at the beginning of this chapter is not a genuine problem, and each of them has been seen to fail. The problem, therefore, remains. There are, however, two further arguments to consider. It may be said that the problem indeed remains but is not susceptible of solution, being a mystery or an example of the absurd. Or it may be said that, although there may be a solution, it is no part of the theologian's task to find it;

it is a problem for logicians and philosophers, not for those whose business it is to contemplate the truths that God has revealed.

The first case might be argued as follows: The problem of evil is a problem about how God has made the world, and his dealings with it. Now God transcends all human power and all human thought, and we ought not to expect to be able to understand him and his works. Any attempt to do so, to probe the mystery by merely human methods of analysis, is impious and shows its folly by resulting in absurdity and self-contradiction. The Christian theologian recognises that all God's dealings with his creation are absurd in this sense, but by the gift of faith the theologian is able to accept this absurdity and to transcend his or own mere rationality. Thus theologians will not expect any solution to the problem of evil. Indeed, they will reject all attempted solutions as so many attempts to limit God to the status of an object for our intellects.

To this argument I reply that it is indeed the case that God's dealings with his creatures transcend our human understanding, and the Christian theologian should reject as impious any attempt to enclose God within the categories of our thinking. But this very point, as will appear in the course of this essay, so far from being a reason for refusing to deal with the problem of evil, is actually the *key* to its rational solution. The problem of evil is not a question about what we are prepared to allow God to do. It is a question about what our language will allow us to say. The existence of evil seems to show that we cannot say that God is good if we want to say that he is omnipotent. Nor can we say that he is omnipotent if we want to say that he is good. However existential one's thought may be, it is necessary to express this thought in language, and to assert one thing is to deny its denial. If, then, it is claimed that to believe in God is to assert both the thing and its denial, there is a problem. There is a problem not because of some invented rigid rules of logic, but because one will not yet have succeeded in saying anything. To succeed in saying something about God is the most elementary task of the theologian, as the word 'theologian' implies.

This, I hope, suffices to show that it is necessary for the theologian to dissolve the problem of evil. It is not merely a task for philosophers. But furthermore, the dealings of God with his creatures do not absolutely transcend the understanding of theologians, for they are people of faith, and faith is not a consent to the absurd but an assent to what is dark and hidden from us only by the weakness of our minds. Faith is not the abdication of knowledge; rather, it remains within the order of knowledge. When we talk about God we are still concerned with an object of knowledge even though our contact with this object is not an act of knowing. It is for this reason that faith can bring us to a kind of understanding of God's dealings with the world, at least sufficient for us to be able to say that God's plan is not one of absurdity.

Two

Metaphysical Preliminaries

Ihave shown that the problem of evil cannot easily be dismissed by the type of argument employed in the last chapter, and I shall now begin to consider the way in which St Thomas deals with the question. For him it is a metaphysical problem that cannot be dissolved except by exposing the metaphysical errors hidden in its formulation. It is clearly important to begin by asking what the word 'evil' means, though this question is frequently omitted in contemporary formulations of the problem. It is often supposed that we all know what evil is, or that at any rate we all recognise that some things, for example extreme pain, are evil, and that the problem can be formulated in terms of such examples. This is, of course, an elementary logical error. Even if all pain is evil, it does not follow that the co-existence of pain and God presents the same problem as the co-existence of evil and God. There is, in fact, a theological 'problem of pain' only because there is a problem of evil, and pain is an evil. For St Thomas, the meaning of the word 'evil' depends upon the meaning of 'good', and an understanding of this depends, in its turn, upon an understanding of 'being'. It is therefore necessary to begin by giving some account of these fundamental metaphysical notions.

Since the main business of this essay is not metaphysics, I have kept this philosophical chapter as short as possible. It is divided into four sections: the first will deal with certain general objections to metaphysical thinking, the second will contain a brief outline of St Thomas' theory of *essence*, the third will deal with *properties*, and the fourth will be a short note on *perfection* and the notion of *cause*. From this, I hope, there will emerge a general outline of St Thomas' metaphysical worldview, which will be sufficient to enable us to follow him through his dissolution of the problem of evil.

Some Misconceptions concerning Metaphysics

Aquinas holds that metaphysics is the study of being. It is the inquiry in which we are concerned with things precisely in so far as they are things.[1] Yet, it might be argued, it appears that there cannot be any such study, for the following reason.

When we define a study or a branch of knowledge, we do so by saying what it is in things that makes them interesting for that study. Thus criminology is defined if we say that things are of interest for this science in so far as they are crimes or have to do with crimes. Similarly, philately is the branch of knowledge for which things are interesting in so far as they are stamps or have to do with stamps. There is no reason why the same thing or event should not be of interest in two different inquiries. Thus the theft of a postage stamp may interest both the criminologist and the philatelist, but it will interest them for different reasons. So long as there are different reasons for being interested in things there are different inquiries. It might be thought that to say that metaphysics is an interest in things in so far as they are things is to give the defining characteristic of metaphysics, as opposed to

---

[1]   Cf. St Thomas' *Commentary on the Metaphysics of Aristotle*, Bk IV, Lect. 1, n. 532.

philately and criminology, but this is, in fact, a mistake. The philatelist and criminologist have different interests in the theft of a valuable stamp. The former is perhaps concerned with the provenance of a particular item in his collection and to him the criminologist's findings can be a matter of indifference; whether, for example, the thief was fully responsible for his actions or mildly insane is of no importance. Similarly the criminologist can be indifferent to just those things that make up the philatelist's interests. It is for this reason that we say that the interests are genuinely different: one can be *abstracted* from the other. This does not mean that one can exist without the other (the theft would not be an interesting or important crime unless the stamp were philatelically interesting) but it means that the pursuit of one inquiry can be accompanied by indifference to the other inquiry. Now it may be a matter of indifference to collectors whether their stamps are stolen stamps or not, but one question that is plainly not a matter of indifference to them is the question of them *being* stamps or *not being* stamps. In so far as they are interested in stamps, they are interested in things being stamps. The study of being, therefore, is not a matter of indifference to the philatelist in the way in which the study of the theft may be. Clearly this same consideration applies to all branches of knowledge. In so far as they are concerned with a certain kind of thing, they are concerned with the things *being* this kind of thing as opposed to *not being* this kind of thing. It thus seems clear that metaphysics is not distinguishable from other sciences; it is not simply that everything that is studied by other sciences is in fact a being, but that these other sciences are specifically concerned with the being of things. On this showing it appears that metaphysics is simply the sum total of all other branches of knowledge.

To this it might be replied that, although other studies are indeed concerned with being (in so far as they are concerned with special ways of being), metaphysics is the study not of the modes and qualifications of being but of being as such. A thing, it might be said, first of all *is*, and then there supervenes upon this being the characteristic of being this or that: being a human being, being a criminal, being a stamp dealer, being a material object, being alive. St Thomas puts just such a view into the mouth of one of his objectors in the *Summa Theologiae*: 'Simply to exist is seemingly most imperfect (the most common of all things).'[2] Metaphysics, it might be claimed, is concerned with the absolute being of things, as opposed to their not being; it leaves to other sciences the concern with the specific differences and qualities of things by which they differ from other things. This notion of absolute being, is, however, unintelligible. It has been said that *being* is a more general characteristic of things than, for example, humanity – in the sense in which *being a crime* is a more general characteristic of an event than *being a theft* or *being a murder*. There is, however, an important difference between the two cases. The more general characteristic, *being a crime*, can be opposed to *not being a crime* in the sense of being something other than a crime, whereas the so-called general characteristic

---

[2]   *Summa Theologiae*, 1a, 4, 1, obj. 3. 'Ipsum esse videtur esse imperfectissimum, cum sit communissimum et recipiens omnium additiones.'

of *being* cannot be opposed to *not being* in the sense of being something other than a being.

It is extremely easy to fall into the trap of thinking of beings as existing in a sort of space of not-being, but this is an illusion. If we compare the statements 'I can see trees' and 'I can see nothing,' it is clear that while 'trees' serves to signify what can be seen, 'nothing' does not have this function. It functions rather in the manner of an adverb than as an object of the verb. Similarly, if we compare 'Flossy is a purple cow' with 'Peter is a human being,' it will be clear that while the first can be split into two independent statements 'Flossy is purple' and 'Flossy is a cow,' the second cannot be split into two independent statements 'Peter is human' and 'Peter is a being.' It is instructive to compare 'Peter is a human being' with 'M. Poujade is a political nonentity.' Just as the latter does not entail 'M. Poujade is a nonentity,' so the former does not entail 'Peter is a being.'

Since, therefore, the study of being cannot be the study of absolute being in the sense criticised above, it remains to be shown that there is any genuine science of metaphysics which is not simply the sum total of all other branches of knowledge. St Thomas accepts, and himself expounds, these criticisms of the notion of being as a highest category or most general characteristic.[3] For him it is not possible to think of things as being, as opposed to thinking of them as nonbeing. In his view no

---

[3]   Cf. *Commentary on the Metaphysics of Aristotle*, Bk I, Lect. 9, n. 139; Bk V, Lect. 9, n. 889; Bk XI, Lect. 1, n. 2170. Cf. also *On the Principles of Nature*, VI.

sense can be made of 'thinking of something as nonbeing'. Things can only be *or be thought of* in so far as they are beings. Of course it is possible to judge or make the statement that, for example, the Brandywine does not exist; but in making this judgement one does not entertain the concept of the Brandywine as non-existent in the sense in which one does entertain the concept of the Brandywine as a river.

But if being is not to be distinguished from not-being or nothing, from what is it to be distinguished? And if it is not to be distinguished from anything, how can we be said to have the notion of being at all? Of course, St Thomas' view of the function of 'nothing', the view that being is distinguished over against nothing and the view that being is not distinguished over against anything, are not alternative views but the same view. There is a sense in which St Thomas is prepared to accept this view, though he prefers the latter formulation of it: he prefers to say that everything is being rather than that anything which is not being is nothing. His solution to the problem involves taking a different starting point. Following and elucidating Aristotle, he begins by saying that for a thing to be is for it to have an essence and that what the essence is depends on what sort of a thing it is. Thus for a human being to be is for him or her to have the essence *humanity*; for a horse to be is, doubtless, for it to have *horseness*. For a human being, to be human is to be *simpliciter* (simply; as in, to be *simply, without qualification*). For a horse, to be a horse is to be *simpliciter*. For a human being, being is opposed, not to nothing, but to being something other than a human being. For a horse, being is opposed to being something other than a horse. When a horse ceases to be a horse it simply ceases to exist. It might seem at first sight that here what might perhaps be called the 'positivist' strain in St Thomas has eliminated metaphysics and the study of *being* altogether: Can we not distinguish being a human being from being something other than a human being (such as a horse) without introducing the notion of *being* at all? To this question one can imagine St Thomas replying: 'Perhaps this is so; let us find out by trying to distinguish being human from being something other than human.' If we pursue this project we discover that while we can readily distinguish being human from, say, being a horse without explicit recourse to the notion of being, as soon as it occurs to us to distinguish being human from, for example, being upside down, or being heavy, certain complications set in.

The logical and metaphysical discussion that follows may seem to be remote from the problem of evil and suffering, and it may therefore be useful to provide a preliminary summary of the whole argument. In the first place, I shall be concerned in the next sections with establishing a pluralistic view of the world. I will show that we cannot simply speak of 'reality' or 'the world' as absolute; there are in fact many things and many different kinds of things. I will show that these different kinds of things provide different contexts of language and knowledge. Then it will appear that in order to under-stand certain highly general words such as 'being', 'good' and 'evil', we have to understand the particular context in which they are being used. I will show that the problem of evil arises because of the mistaken assumption that God is one among many other kinds of things – that, in fact, it is a typically metaphysical muddle due to the uncontrolled application of words outside their due contexts. Finally, I will show that there is such a thing as the controlled application of words outside their native contexts and that not only can we deny that God can be said to be evil, but we can assert that he is good.

The Notion of Essence in St Thomas' Metaphysics

According to St Thomas, existence belongs only to essences. As it stands this statement might possibly mislead the reader into thinking that St Thomas believed that what was not an essence laboured under the disadvantage of not existing. In order to avoid this sort of misapprehension it will be helpful to perform the operation known to modern philosophers as translating from the material to the formal mode. Instead of asking what can be said to exist, we might ask to what subjects can the predicate 'exists' properly be attached. St Thomas' answer is that phrases whose meaning is given by a *definitio* (definition) are the only proper candidates for the predicate 'exists'.[4] There are certain further requirements, such as that the phrase should be grammatically concrete and not abstract, but this, which has to do with the distinction of essence and *suppositum* (an individual substance) will be considered later. Another

---

[4]   Cf. *Commentary on the Metaphysics of Aristotle*, Bk VII, Lect. 12, n. 1537. Cf. also *On Being and Essence*, Chapter 2, n. 5.

qualification to be noticed is that this statement as it stands would rule out the sentence 'God exists' and it might be thought that it would be better to re-formulate it to meet this latter case. It is one of the most striking differences between St Thomas and later writers in the scholastic tradition that he never seeks to formulate generalisations large enough to include God as well as creatures. God does not enter his thought either as an exception to, or a particular case of, any rule. God transcends all such rules.

In St Thomas' view it is proper to say 'The human being exists' but not proper to say 'The Englishman exists.' This sounds a somewhat startling doctrine at first, but it must be recognised that it does not mean that we are mistaken in supposing that there are Englishmen, or that men who become naturalised Englishmen suddenly vanish. Neither does it mean that we ought never to say 'Englishmen exist.' All that it means is that whereas human beings exist precisely because they are human beings, we cannot say that Englishmen exist precisely because they are Englishmen. In other words existence is *proper* to human beings as such, whereas it is not *proper* to Englishmen as such. The doctrine that 'Human beings exist' is a proper sentence, while 'Englishmen exist' is not, is parallel to the assertion that 'Communists believe in Marxism' is a proper sentence, whereas 'Texans believe in Marxism' is not; and this latter assertion would be true even if all Texans in fact believed in Marxism.

It may still be felt that the doctrine is obscure in that it seems just as easy to *define* the word 'Englishman' as it is to define the phrase 'human being'. To this, however, it must be replied that there is in fact no definition of 'Englishman'. This does not mean that its meaning cannot be explained, but that its meaning cannot be explained in the special way for which St Thomas reserves the name *definitio*, for not every explanation of the meaning of a word is, for him, a definition. Briefly, a definition, in his sense, is obtained by differentiating a genus, as, for example, when we say that a human being is the kind of animal that is rational. Now it might appear that to say that an Englishman is the kind of man that is English is to differentiate the genus *man* by means of the differentia *English*. This, however, is not the case, for being English is not a differentia of being a man, but rather accidental to it. To say that someone is an Englishman is not to explain precisely *how he is a man*. In fact there is no way of explaining how anything is a man; all men are meant in the same way because man is a species and not a genus. When I say that something is a rational animal, I am explaining in what way the thing is an animal. There is no species *animal*, at any rate not in the sense in which the word is used in defining human beings. Having been told that something is an animal one waits for the account to be completed. Genus words, such as 'animal', are incomplete in their meaning. One needs to be told whether the animality in question is rational animality, or animality in some other sense. The genus does not yet fully determine what it is for the thing to be. To say of an Englishman that he is an animal is partly to say what he is. Porphyry, in an illuminating phrase, says that in a definition the differentia must be such as to bring the genus to *being* (*ad esse conducit*) but an accident supervenes upon an already constituted thing. An Englishman exists not because he is an Englishman but because he is a man; the accident of being English could be lost without his ceasing to exist.

Thus, says St Thomas, a human being is an *ens secundum se* (a being in virtue of what it is itself); whereas an Englishman is an *ens secundum accidens* (a being according to accident). Of course there is a difference between being a man and being white although both are ways of being *secundum se*. For to be a man is to be *simpliciter*. If you say 'George is a man,' you say the same as if you had said 'George exists,' whereas to be white is not to be *simpliciter* but to be *thus*. To say that George is white is not to say that George exists. It is to say that George exists whitely. From this consideration there stems the whole discussion of the categories which is fundamental to St Thomas' metaphysics. It is because of his theory of the categories that he is able to answer the question, 'With what is *being* contrasted?' He does not say that being is contrasted with not-being (although he is prepared to admit a sense in which being can be said not to be contrasted with anything). Nor does he say that all we can speak of are specifically different kinds of beings, contrasting one sort of thing with another. He contrasts being in the primary sense (substance, or being *simpliciter*) with being in secondary senses (accidents). These secondary senses are dependent upon the primary sense but not reducible to it.

This may best be brought out by showing the difference between *ens* in the primary sense and *ens secundum accidens*. All statements about *entia secundum accidens* can be translated into statements about *entia secundum se*. *Entia secundum accidens*, that is to say, are logical constructions out of *entia secundum se*. Statements about accidents, on the other hand, cannot be translated into statements about substances. Statements about accidents could not be *true* unless there were some statements about substances that were true. Thus no statements about justice could be true, or even false, unless it were true that some human or angel or God were just, and in this sense accidents do depend on substance; their whole *esse* (being) is *inesse* (being-in). For present purposes there is no need to say more about the doctrine of the categories, but I must go a little further into the matter of definition.

To define something, to give its essence, is not to say what it is like; it is to say what it is. This may be explained as follows. In an intelligent discussion upon any topic the participants may disagree a good deal, but they will ordinarily be in agreement about what it is that they are discussing. Sometimes they lack this fundamental agreement and we say that they are at cross-purposes. Because we do not commonly *say* what we think the topic of discussion is, but rather *show* it by what we say, it *dawns* upon us that disputants are at cross-purposes. To grasp the essence, what the discussion is about, is, in the intellectual sphere, the same sort of thing as to see an object in the sensitive sphere; it is a beginning. Without it one cannot start action in the one case or thought in the other. Thus if Fred says that the mass of the carbon dioxide molecule is fifty times that of the hydrogen molecule, he is wrong. He has made a mistake in the atomic weights involved, and we might point this out. But if he speaks of the carbon dioxide molecule as being at 30 degrees centigrade, then we might begin to think that he did not know *what* he was talking about. He *shows* that he does not know what a molecule is, for molecules cannot either be or fail to be at 30 degrees centigrade; they do not have temperature. Molecules are neither hot nor cold, just as they are neither hard nor soft, neither affectionate nor disagreeable. To know what a molecule is is to know that to speak about its temperature is to speak inappropriately.

Of course there is nothing unlawful about speaking inappropriately, and for certain purposes, notably for certain logicians' purposes, someone might want to treat the statement 'The molecule is at 30 degrees centigrade' or 'The table is hungry' as straightforwardly false in the same way as, for example, 'Water at normal pressure boils at 30 degrees centigrade' is false. My purpose is simply to draw attention to a difference, even if this difference may legitimately be overlooked by logicians. However, there is a danger that, having overlooked such differences, the logician may turn metaphysician and regard this logical 'language' as especially appropriate for expressing what is really the case (as did the philosophers now referred to as Logical Atomists). If, for example, a statement is only regarded as respectable in so far as it can be expressed in the symbolism of *Principia Mathematica*, then there is clearly no place for a notion of essence, since the only restrictions upon proposition formation will be those necessitated by type differences.

It is common today for philosophers to dismiss the Logical Atomists' quest for an 'ideal language' as summarily as the Logical Atomists themselves dismissed the idea of essence. In this I think the contemporary analysts are in error. The Aristotelian theory of essence which I would maintain to be correct, is, in fact, an 'ideal language' theory. And it is one that can account for the manifest search for an ideal language on the part of the working scientist while eluding the objections that inevitably overthrew the theory that ordinary language could be accounted for in terms of logical constructions from *Principia Mathematica* propositions with 'logically proper names' substituted for variables. It is also common for modern scholastics to neglect the theory of essence, passing over the problems with glib quotations about the difficulty of knowing the essence of a house-fly. For this reason it is worth pointing out that if the theory of essence is mistaken, if there are not 'natural kinds' as a matter of the structure of the world and not simply as a matter of our linguistic decision, then the whole of St Thomas' writings, theological as well as philosophical, are of merely historical interest, being nothing but an elaborate tissue of errors.

The essence, the definition of a thing, determines what can appropriately be said of it. It is because of what a human being is (a rational animal) that we can speak of human beings appropriately as angry or not angry. We can, indeed, speak of the sea as angry or calm, but only in a metaphorical sense, because the sea is not the *kind of thing* that can properly be said to be or not to be angry. In saying, then, that existence belongs to the essence,

St Thomas is saying that reality is not made up of facts, or phenomena, or collections of phenomena, or of 'something I know not what' behind appearances, but of topics of discussion. For each kind of thing there is its appropriate language (it has an essence) and this language can be used to make true or false statements, statements with point (it exists). It is perhaps worth noting here that according to St Thomas' metaphysical doctrine, the fact that there are many individuals of one species is not expressed by saying that the essence is received in many different exemplifications. The individualisation of the essence is not due to the composition of the essence with something else. In particular, it has not to do with the composition of essence and existence. It is due to the composition *within* the essence of matter and form. As St Thomas writes: 'The existence of a composite substance is neither form alone nor matter alone but is rather composed of these. The essence is that according to which the thing is said to exist; hence, it is right that the essence by which a thing is denominated a being is neither form alone nor matter alone but both, albeit that existence of this kind is caused by the form.'[5]

It is not the essence of human beings that is individualised, but rather it is of the essence of human beings that they are individual. The essence is 'what it takes' for a thing to exist, and one of the things that it takes for a human being to exist is that he or she should be an individual. It is certainly not the case that, for St Thomas, all that exists is individual and concrete. For him, angels

---

[5]   *On Being and Essence*, Chapter 2, n. 6.

are not, in this sense, individuals, and God is not an individual. St Thomas believes as much as any Platonist in subsistent forms; he merely denies that if the forms of material things subsisted they could be the essences of the things. His case against the Platonist is that such subsistent forms would not be relevant to the being and intelligibility of the only things that we can adequately understand (i.e. material things). He believed that, in fact, the forms of some material things (people) did subsist, but he also believed that it is not possible that the *essence* of people (humanity) should subsist immaterially.

The grammatical device by which we speak both of things and of their essences (the use of concrete and abstract nouns) serves two purposes. On the one hand, it reflects the distinction of matter and form within the essence which accounts for plurality within a species. Thus 'human being' has a plural, but 'humanity' has not. Hence there is no danger of confusing such a statement as 'Many human beings have the same humanity,' which advertises itself as a logical or metaphysical statement, with such a statement as 'Many human beings have the same house'; for the latter can be denied by saying that they have different *houses* whereas it could not be said that they have different *humanities*. On the other hand the distinction of abstract and concrete is also used to express the distinction of *suppositum* and nature, that is to say the distinction between what can be said of a human being and what can be said of a human being precisely in so far as he or she is a human being. So long as there is such a distinction (i.e. so long as a thing has accidents as well as its essence), there is a place for such a difference. Nevertheless, although there must remain a distinction of *suppositum* and nature even in the angels, in whom there is no distinction of matter and form, it is not easy to say whether the device of abstract and concrete nouns still has a place in speaking of angels or not. Should 'Raphael' always be replaceable by 'Raphaelity' in order to bring out the fact that Raphael is not a concrete individual of a species, or should the difference be maintained to bring out the distinction between, for example, Raphael and his acts? The fact is, of course, that since we are here using language outside its native context of material things, there can be no simple solution to such a problem.

It will be clear that, for St Thomas, all essences exist; it makes no sense to speak of an essence not existing. This is evident from the fact that he regards the statement that Harry is a human being (which tells us what Harry is) as a statement that Harry is *simpliciter*. If there were such a thing as Harry's essence deprived of existence, this state of affairs could only be represented by saying that Harry is *not* a human being. But since, in St Thomas' view, the proper name 'Harry' signifies human nature and differs from 'human being' only in its *modus significandi* (mode of signifying) not in its *significatum* (thing signified), the sentence 'Harry is not a human being' would be self-contradictory. Hence the statement that Harry is a human being, which states that Harry exists, cannot be false. It does not, however, follow from this that the statement that Harry exists can never be false, for 'Harry is a human being' can fail to be a true statement (thus rendering it false that Harry exists) without being a false statement. This would be the case if it is not a statement at all, but merely a linguistic rule determining the meaning of the noun 'Harry'. When a thing ceases to exist, therefore, one is not left with an essence lacking existence; one is left with a meaningful word that is not the name of anything. Thus the difference between Harry existing and Harry not existing is that while in both cases one can construct with the name 'Harry' a number of meaningful sentences such as 'Harry is hungry' or 'Harry is not hungry,' all authorised by 'Harry is a human being' in so far as it is a *rule* governing the significance of 'Harry', it is only in the former case that such sentences will have point. In the former case they can at least be false, since they are statements founded upon the fundamental *statement* 'Harry is a human being,' which tells us that he exists.

Of course, a mere account of the meaning of a word, which is not at the same time a definition, is secondary to a genuine definition, in that when one invents a word one is *playing at* defining. A definition is not the meaning of a word *plus* the qualification that the word names something (meaning, with an existence proviso) any more than a human being is a statue *plus* life. Saying what a human being is is not like saying what a hobbit is, with the additional proviso that there are humans but no hobbits. Rather, in saying what a hobbit is one is pretending to do what one does in saying what a human being is. There are not two or three kinds of existence – real existence for people, imaginary existence for hobbits, mathematical existence for triangles, etc. Hobbits do not have a fictional sort of existence; it is a fiction that hobbits have a perfectly ordinary sort of existence. (Of course there are different senses of the word 'exists', notably the different sense in which substances and accidents are said to exist, but that is not what is in question here.)

Properties

So far I have been concerned with particular essences, and it will be clear from what I have said that these are prior to the *world* or to *reality*. There are philosophers for whom the world is ultimate, a sort of wall of reality upon which are drawn the various shapes of things. Such philosophers strive to get behind the differences of things to a common reality that they all share. For St Thomas, however, the multitude of things that there are do not have it in common that they are ultimately parts of a single world. They can be spoken of as having something in common only because they all owe their existence to one creator who altogether transcends the world. Thus when St Thomas asks himself whether there is, in fact, one world, he replies that there is because it is created by the wisdom of God.[6] So the fact that there is a *world* is, for him, less obvious than the fact that there is a *God*, and this in its turn is less obvious than the fact that there are *things*. We have already seen something of this in the fact that St Thomas does not attempt to answer the question 'What is the relation of language (or thought) to reality?' As Wittgenstein clearly saw, there is

---

[6] Cf. *Summa Theologiae*, 1a, 47, 3.

no language in which to answer this question. Instead St Thomas asks 'How can we talk about this, and about that ...?' To ask this is to ask for essences, and, in his metaphysics, puzzles about the relation of language to reality are eliminated by the principle that existence simply belongs to essence.

In order, now, to pass on from the notion of being to that of goodness, I shall need to consider this secondary idea of the *world*. I must consider, in fact, the togetherness of things, what St Thomas calls the unity of *order* amongst things.

He writes: 'For this world is called one by the unity of order, whereby some things are ordered to others.'[7] There could be no greater contrast than that between this statement and the theory that statements are ultimately 'true about the world'. We have seen what a thing must have in order to exist at all (to be *simpliciter*), that is its essence; we must now consider what it must have in order to belong to its world.

I emphasised in the previous section that to give the essence of a thing is simply to state *what* it is; it is not to say anything about it, in the ordinary sense. Thus, to say that Harry is a rational animal is only to say that he may appropriately be said to be sane or insane, etc.; it is not to say that he *is* sane or that he *is* insane. One knows no facts about a thing from its definition. As far as the essence goes, it seems, rational animals are as much

---

7   *Summa Theologiae*, 1a, 47, 3. 'Mundus enim iste unus dicitur *unitate ordinis*, secundum quod quaedam ad alia ordinantur.'

rational animals if they have never had the use of their reason as if they were the greatest of philosophers. Thus, though from the definition we can say that all human beings are rational, we can certainly not say that all human beings are sane. It would seem, therefore, that apart from what is essential to a thing, everything else is merely accidental. But this seems a hard saying. A human being is clearly no more of a human being for being sunburned, or not being sunburned, but there does seem to be *some* sense in which we can say that he or she is more of a human being for being sane rather than insane. We speak of 'inhuman cruelty' as though someone might become slightly less human by doing certain things.

In order to elucidate this we must briefly consider the notion of property (what St Thomas calls *proprietas*). For St Thomas, properties are characteristics that are neither strictly essential to a thing nor yet merely accidental. This notion seems, at first sight, a difficult one. The proposition that X has the characteristic Y seems to be either an analytic proposition (when part of what is meant by being X is having Y) or a contingent synthetic proposition (when it might just as well be the case that X has not got Y). There is a classical philosophical problem here: Our science is either to consist of a collection of synthetic propositions which just so happen to be true, with no intelligible necessity about them, or else it is to consist of a formal structure of analytic propositions which cannot be false but which are also independent of experience. We should like to say that our knowledge of things is both experiential and in some sense necessary, but this seems difficult. Kant, as is well known, attempted to solve this problem with the aid of synthetic a priori propositions.[8] Aristotle and St Thomas meet the difficulty in another way. Briefly, for them, the scientific study of things is concerned with their properties, and properties are characteristics that a thing must necessarily have *ut in pluribus* (for the most part).

This last clause presupposes an important logical principle which I shall call the 'Logical stringency of "most"'. It is commonly supposed that if it is true that some X is not Y, then it is possible that no X is Y; for if some X is not Y then it is not necessary that all X is Y, and so long as this latter proposition is not necessary then it may be the case that no X is Y. Against this, however, it can be shown that in some cases, although some X is not Y, and although it is therefore not necessary that *all* X is Y, nevertheless, not only is it necessary that *some* X is Y, but that *most* X is Y. The whole theory of 'nature' in the material world, with its correlative notion of 'chance'; St Thomas' theory of causation with its correlative idea of *impedance*;[9] the constant qualification of any generalised statement about the behaviour of material things by the phrase *saltem ut in pluribus* (at least for the most part)[10] all show that St Thomas recognised the logical force of 'most' statements. A simple example may serve to elucidate the point. Some card-

8   Cf. the Introduction to the *Critique of Pure Reason*.
9   Cf. *Summa Theologiae*, 1a2ae, 75, 1, ad 2. Cf. also *On Memory and Recollection*, Lect. 6, n. 384; *Commentary on the Metaphysics of Aristotle*, VI, Lect. 3, n. 1193.
10 See especially the discussion in St Thomas' *Commentary on Aristotle's Physics*, II, Lect. 12, nn. 253–254.

players cheat, but it is logically necessary that most card-players do not cheat. The reason for this is that in a world in which most card-players cheated there could not be any card games at all. Wittgenstein rediscovered this point:

> 'What sometimes happens might always happen.'—What kind of proposition is that? It is like the following: If 'F(a)' makes sense '(x)F(x)' makes sense.
>
> 'If it is possible for someone to make a false move in some game then it might be possible for everybody to make nothing but false moves in every game'—Thus we are under a temptation to misunderstand the logic of our expressions here, to give an incorrect account of the use of our words.
>
> Orders are sometimes not obeyed. But how would it look if no orders were *ever* obeyed? The concept 'order' would have lost its purpose.[11]

I am not, of course, suggesting that the phrase 'card-player' would lose its meaning merely because there were no games of cards in the world. But it would lose its meaning if there *could not be* any games of cards in the world; and this would be the case if most card-players cheated most of the time. It is not a question of a *word* losing its purpose, but of a *concept* losing its purpose (i.e. of a word losing its meaning). A certain small amount of cheating or of careless play can be tolerated, but once the thing becomes normal, the game has disappeared. In

---

[11] *Philosophical Investigations*, trans. G.E.M. Anscombe (Oxford: Basil Blackwell, 1968), § 345.

much the same way, society can tolerate a certain small amount of crime, but the proposition 'most members of society are not criminals most of the time' is a logically necessary one. It might be said that, for St Thomas, the world is neither rigidly governed by scientific laws, nor is it anarchical: it is regular and ordered and law-abiding, for the most part, but it allows for occasional disorders, occasional exceptions, occasional monsters.

Let us take, for example, the case of the human being. The essence of the human being is to be a rational animal; this is all that it needs in order to be, but this is by no means all that scientific investigators can say about a human being. Admittedly, anything else that they attribute to a human being may be falsified in a particular case, but there are many things that cannot but be true *ut in pluribus*. It will be remembered that the definition 'rational animal' tells us the kind of language that can be used in speaking of a human being, as opposed, let us say, to that used in speaking of a cow or a stone or the sun. The definition authorises a certain kind of appropriate talk, and in fact we only discover the definition by examining the talk that we use. As I have said, we arrive at the essence by asking what is *shown* by what is said about a thing. Now it is clearly possible for someone to be born who is incapable of communicating with other people by speech or in any other way, but let us suppose that most people are born in this condition. Let us, in short, examine a world in which the proposition 'Most people can communicate with one another' is untrue. Clearly in such a world we should have no place for most of the words that are characteristically authorised by the definition of 'human'. The words 'disbelief', 'unintelligent', 'crime', 'unwitting', 'desperate', 'unjust', and so on, would have no use and hence the definition would be empty of meaning. Of course we are here thinking of the *via judicii* (way of judgement; as in deductive reasoning) not the *via inventionis* (way of discovery; as in inductive reasoning). In the latter case we find characteristics that are properties empirically, simply by observing what is usually the case. By the *via judicii* we show that it is no mere empirical generalisation that most people can think, or that most of them can walk.

When we say that certain exceptions to the rules can be tolerated we do not mean that there is an element, but fortunately only a small element, of lawlessness in things. An exception to a general rule is not an occasion for a shrug; on the contrary, for Aristotle, it is the occasion of *admiratio* (wonder, in St Thomas' Latin), the root of all scientific investigation. It is when one finds someone who cannot think, in spite of the fact that it is a property of people to think, that one begins to investigate the cause of this oddity, and in this way a science begins. Children ask questions like 'Why does the sun shine?' to which one can reasonably and adequately reply, 'Why shouldn't it shine?', and this disposes of the question. But a question is a scientific one when this move can be countered by an appeal to what is normal and proper: 'Why is this man insane?' 'Well, why shouldn't he be insane?' 'Because he is a man, and it is a property of humans to be sane.' In general, if 'Most Xs are Y' is a necessary proposition (i.e. if being Y is a property of X), then a case in which X is not Y calls for *explanation*. This

God and Evil

is the basis of the Aristotelian notion of causation: a thing is either *natural* or else it has a cause. Of course the notion of cause is later extended so that it is possible even to talk of what is natural as caused, but basically cause is the complement of nature. Enough has perhaps been said to indicate the place of properties in an Aristotelian picture of the world; I am now in a position to use this notion to define *perfection* and *imperfection*. Briefly, a perfect X is an X that has all its properties; an imperfect X lacks one or more of its properties.

Perfection and Causality

To say that a certain characteristic is not merely accidental to, but is a property of, say, a dog, is to say that to have this characteristic is to be 'more canine'. The properties of a dog are those characteristics that make for the perfection of dogness in the dog. Of course, there is a fundamental sense in which a thing simply is a dog or is not; its essence is not susceptible of more and less. But there is also this other sense in which one dog can be more doggy than another. It is for this reason that St Thomas speaks of perfection as in a special sense an actualisation of the perfected thing – although in a general sense *any* accidental determination is an actualisation. 'For we call things perfect when they have achieved actuality (a perfect thing being that in which nothing required by its particular mode of perfection fails to exist).'[12] Thus when John is sunburned, he

---

[12] Cf. *Summa Theologiae*, 1a, 4, 1.

becomes actually brown after being merely potentially brown; he has achieved a certain actualisation. But he has not achieved an actualisation *secundum modum suae perfectionis* (according to the mode *of his* perfection). He may have become perfectly brown, but he has not *eo ipso* become perfectly a human being. On the other hand, when children learn to talk, they have not simply actualised a certain accidental capacity; they have also actualised themselves. They have become 'more human'. And just as to be human is to be *simpliciter*, so also for a human being, to become more human is to become more perfect *simpliciter*.

Perfection is, for St Thomas, intimately associated with goodness, but he always begins his consideration of goodness from the point of view of appetite. A good thing is, in the first place, a thing that is desirable; it is what gives purpose to activity and is that in which satisfaction is attained. Since goodness is what is desired or sought for, it is clear that the purpose of an activity is more properly and immediately to be called good than the means by which the purpose is attained. Means as such derive their desirability from the desirability of the end, but the latter does not depend on the former. When we speak of something as a 'necessity', we normally mean that it is not valuable for its own sake but rather as a means to something which is valuable for its own sake. This is of interest to us because it brings out the connection between goodness and perfection: there is some point in having defective necessities, but absolutely no point in having defective luxuries. Even stale bread will do to save someone from starvation, but a bad poem is quite worthless, for the only value of a poem is the value it has in itself. Thus the thing that is good in itself must be perfect, whereas the thing that is only good in relation to something else may be imperfect.

St Thomas explains the connections between goodness, perfection and being in a short passage which is worth quoting in full:

> It is not the same thing to call something a *being* without qualification, and to call it *good* without qualification. For to call something a being is to say that it really exists; and, since we use the word 'real' as the opposite of 'merely possible', something can be called a being as soon as it can no longer be said to be merely possible.
>
> But a thing ceases to be merely possible as soon as it is *what* it is. Hence it is in virtue of this substantial being that a thing is called a being. Any other reality over and above its substantial being does not make us call it a being without qualification; we say rather that in virtue of such superadded reality it is *in some respect*. For example, to be white is not to be simply, but to be in some respect. A thing is not white as opposed to being merely potential; before it was white it already really existed.
>
> But to call a thing good is to call it perfect and desirable, and this implies completeness and *finish*. It is when the thing has got its final perfection that we call it good without qualification. Before then, when it has not got the final perfection that it

needs—even though it has a certain perfection in as much as it exists at all—it is not called good simply speaking; it is merely said to be perfect in a certain respect.

Thus by the first being that a thing has—its substantial being—it is called a being and it is called good: but it is called a being simply without qualification, whereas it is a good thing only in a certain respect. On the other hand by the final reality that a thing acquires it is said to *be* only in a certain respect, but to be *good* without qualification.[13]

Thus the thing that is in the first place good, the thing that is, simply speaking, desirable is the thing that not only has its substantial form but that has in addition to this the superadded accidental forms of its properties; and this is an *ens secundum accidens*, for a thing does not exist in virtue of having its properties, but only in virtue of having its essence.

I have spoken of the thing complete with its properties as desirable, and the question naturally arises 'Desirable to whom?' Anything might be desirable to a person under appropriate conditions. Here we must return to our distinction between desiring a thing for its own sake and desiring it as a means to some ulterior end. A thing is called good, absolutely speaking, if it is desirable to one who desires it for its own sake. If it is desired as a means, it is only relatively good. And at this point the notion of

---

[13] *Summa Theologiae*, 1a, 5, 1, ad 1.

perfection becomes entwined with that of causality. When I use a stone to hammer in a nail, I give the stone a function; it fulfils some purpose of mine; it performs a function in the context of my life. The stone has been endowed with a new norm of perfection. Hitherto it was only a good or bad stone; now *besides this* it is either good or bad for my purposes. We can distinguish between what makes a stone a good stone and what makes it good for hammering. Yet suppose that instead of picking up a stone to hammer in my nail I had brought into being a hammer. The situation would now be different: we cannot distinguish between what makes a hammer a good hammer and what makes it good for hammering. Its perfection as a hammer just is its perfection as a hammerer. Now, of course, I cannot in fact bring a hammer into being. A hammer is an artificial thing, an *ens secundum accidens*; it does not exist in virtue of being a hammer but in virtue of being wood and metal, etc. In fact, to make a hammer and to pick up a stone are two activities that only differ in that the former is more complex; neither of them really involves bringing a new thing into being. For this reason, in spite of what I have said, it is really possible to distinguish, even in the case of a hammer, between its goodness as a thing (wood and metal) and its goodness for hammering.

An efficient cause brings an *ens secundum se* into being, and for this reason the perfection of the thing brought into being is due to the efficient cause. The perfection is due to the operation of the effect acting precisely in virtue of its efficient cause. It is, on the other hand, necessary to distinguish between the end of the cause and the end of the effect. The end of the cause is the being of the effect not precisely in its perfection. Nevertheless, there is an order of finality between the agent and the perfection of the effect precisely because the agent desires the effect for its own sake. It is indeed the same thing for an agent A to desire an effect B for B's sake, and to desire it for A's sake; it is this that defines A as the efficient cause of B. We distinguish desiring B for its own sake, not against desiring it for A's sake, but against desiring it for the sake of some other thing which *makes use of it* when it is already constituted. The difference between the coming to be of an effect and its perfection is that the coming to be is the work solely of the efficient cause, whereas the perfection is due to the effect itself and is only the work of the efficient cause *because* of this. As St Thomas puts it:

> Where there are several agents in order, the second always acts in virtue of the first; for the first agent moves the second to act.[14]

> A, B, and C are three ordered causes so that C is the last, which exercises an operation. It is then an established fact that C exercises an operation by its own power, and it is by the power of B and, more than that, by the power of A that C can do this by its own power. Hence, if it is asked why C operates, the answer is by its own power. And if it asked why by its own power, it is on account of the power of B.[15]

---

[14] *Summa Theologiae*, 1a, 105, 5.
[15] *Commentary on the Sentences of Peter Lombard*, Bk I, d. 37, 1, 1, ad 4.

This is the natural conclusion from St Thomas' principle that the purpose of everything is its operation,[16] for it follows that to intend that something shall be is to intend that it shall operate; and to fulfil this intention is to cause the thing to operate.

It will be clear from what I have said that the cause of B must be of a different order from B. (This same principle is expressed in another field by saying that the explanation is of a higher logical order than the explained.) That is to say, when, for example, we look for the efficient cause that brings into being a dog, we cannot be looking for another dog. According to Aristotle and St Thomas, it is a dog *and the sun* that cause the generation of a dog. The reason for thinking this is that if you are puzzled by the existence of a dog, your puzzlement is in no way reduced if you are told that there is *another* dog.

> Of two things in the same species one cannot directly cause the other's form as such, since it would then be the cause of its own form, which is essentially the same as the form of the other; but it can be the cause of this form for as much as it is in matter—in other words, it may be the cause that 'this matter' receives 'this form.' And this is to be the cause of 'becoming,' as when man begets man, and fire causes fire.[17]

---

16   Cf. *Summa Theologiae*, 1a, 105, 5.
17   *Summa Theologiae*, 1a, 104, 1. 'Si aliqua duo sunt eiusdem speciei, unum non potest esse per se causa formae alterius, inquantum est talis forma: quia sic esset causa formae propriae, cum sit eadem ratio utriusque. Sed potest esse causa huiusmodi forma secundum quod

If the one dog were an adequate explanation of the other, why should it not be an adequate explanation for itself? Why bring in another dog at all? For St Thomas, what he calls 'univocal causality' (in which one member of a species causes another member of the same species to exist) always presupposes 'analogical causality', in which the cause is a different kind of thing from the thing caused.

> Whereas when we are concerned with *predications*, the equivocal use of a predicate presupposes its univocal use, when we are concerned with *activities*, the action of an univocal agent presupposes the action of a non-univocal agent. For the non-univocal agent is the universal cause of the whole species (as the sun is the cause of the generation of all people), but the univocal agent is not the cause of the whole species (for otherwise it would be the cause of itself, since it belongs to the species); rather, it is the particular cause with respect to this individual which is constituted as belonging to the species. The universal cause of the whole species is therefore not an univocal agent; but the universal cause is prior to the particular one.

> This universal agent, although it is not univocal is nevertheless not altogether equivocal, otherwise it would not produce something like itself. But it could be called an 'analogical agent', borrowing a

est in materia, idest quod haec materia acquirat hanc formam. Et hoc est esse causa secundum fieri; sicut cum homo generat hominem et ignis ignem.'

47

term from logic in which we speak of an univocal predication as presupposing a primary predication of being which is not univocal but analogical.[18]

Thus as B achieves its own perfection in performing its operations, there is a sense in which it can be said to be achieving a perfection of its efficient cause A, though it must be recognised that the *achieving* is all on the side of B. The agent A is not affected or changed in any way by the change wrought in B.

This notion of a perfection of A that is realised in B may seem a very difficult one, but in fact it is this that constitutes A as cause of B. An agent (an agent or efficient cause) just is a thing that realises a perfection of itself in something else. We tend to think of the achievement of a perfection as always associated with a change. We tend to think of an active thing as something that moves quickly, as opposed to a still or inactive thing. But for St Thomas movement and activity are actually opposed to each other: movement is a sign not of activity but of passivity. Causes as such stay still; it is effects that move. 'The more immovable certain things are, the more are they the cause of those things which are most movable.'[19] This realisation of a perfection of the agent in the effect can be expressed by saying 'What a thing produces reflects what it is.'[20]

[18] *Summa Theologiae*, 1a, 13, 5, ad 1.
[19] *Summa Theologiae*, 1a, 115, 3.
[20] *Summa Theologiae*, 1a, 4, 3. 'Cum enim omne agens agat sibi simile inquantum est agens.'

The resemblance between agent and effect is not, however, one of sharing in the same form, for the perfection of the thing caused is its perfection as a thing, whereas for the agent it is its perfection *inquantum est agens* (inasmuch as it is an agent). The work of an artist will, in its perfection, be characteristically human, but those same features which are the properly human perfections of the work of a human being cannot be transferred to the artist as a human being in order to perfect *him or her*. It would be a naive error to suppose that a human artefact and a human child shared in some common feature or characteristic of being human, as a red carpet and a red pencil do share in the common feature of being red. The word 'human' in this case is used analogically, while the word 'red' is used univocally.

This must suffice for a very general and brief account of St Thomas' notions of being, essence, perfection, goodness and causal action. I hope that with the aid of the worldview that has thus been sketched we may be able to state clearly the definitive solution that St Thomas offers to the problem of the reality of evil in the world created by God.

THREE

Good and Evil

> Of a pair of opposites, one is understood by means of the
> other, as darkness is understood in terms of light; so we come
> to understand what evil is by considering good.[1]

The Analogical Use of 'Good'

We have seen that a good X is an X with all its properties,
and a good Y is a Y with all *its* properties. Where X and
Y are words with different meanings, the properties of X
will not be the same as the properties of Y, and hence a
good Y will not necessarily have properties in common
with a good X. Clearly, then, it is useless to seek for some
characteristic that good Xs have in common with good
Ys, in virtue of which we call them both good. One way
of putting this is to say that 'good' is a contextually
dependent word. In other words, when we say that
something is a good X, the sense of the word 'good' is not
independent of the meaning of 'X'. We saw something
similar in the case of the word 'exists'. 'George exists'
says what is said by 'George is human,' whereas 'Fido
exists' says what is said by 'Fido is a dog.' Thus we can
say that the sense of 'exists' is also contextually
dependent; it is not independent of the meaning of its
subject. We have seen that *all* predicates must stand in a
certain relation to the meaning of their subjects if they are
to be appropriate; but we are now dealing with words
whose sense (and not merely whose appropriateness) is
dependent on the meaning of their subjects.

---

[1] *Summa Theologiae*, 1a, 48, 1.

Contextual dependence is not peculiar to metaphysical words such as 'good' and 'exists'. It is also found, for example, in mathematical functions such as 'half', 'logarithm' and 'square root'. There is no such thing as the characteristic of a number in virtue of which it is a square root. The similarity between 'The square root of X' and 'The good qualitites of X' is that one cannot use either of these expressions as nouns whose meanings are understood unless one knows the meaning of X. Some have thought that the similarity extends further than this. They notice that although the expression 'The square root of X' cannot be understood without under-standing the meaning of X, nevertheless the expression 'square root' can be used as a noun, and many things can be said about square roots without any reference to what they are the square roots of. For example, we can say, 'Not all square roots are the squares of cube roots.' They are then led to believe that we can talk in a similar way about goodness without any reference to the things that are good. This mistake arises from taking too seriously an accidental similarity between the logical behaviour of metaphysical words and mathematical functions. The similarity is not due to the fact that, for example, goodness is a kind of function, but to the fact that both goodness and being a square root are contextually dependent characteristics. The close connection between mathematical and metaphysical language is emphasised by St Thomas's famous doctrine that such words as 'good' are predicated *secundum analogiam idest secundum proportionem* (according to an analogy, i.e. according to proportion) and in some early works he uses mathematical illustrations to show what he means by 'proportion'.[2] His point here is, of course, to bring out the difference between a function and, for example, a number, and to suggest that there is a similar difference between predicates like 'good' and univocal predicates like 'animal'. There are, nevertheless, fundamental dissimilarities between functions and numbers, which make the illustration limp. For example, square roots or doubles are just as conceptually simple as numbers. There are no such similarities between ultimately analogical words like 'good' and univocal words. Perhaps it was because he foresaw the misunderstandings that his earlier treatment might lead to, that St Thomas in the *Summa Theologiae*, and generally in his later works,[3] avoids mathematical illustrations. Another class of words that resemble metaphysical terms in being contextually dependent are words such as 'small', 'large', 'complete', and 'typical'. The characteristics in virtue of which something is said to be a typical industrial town are quite different from those in virtue of which something is said to be a typical Siamese cat.

The fundamental difference between contextually dependent and independent words is that certain inferences which are permissible in the latter case are not permissible in the former. From the fact that all red pencils, *qua* red, are coloured, it is a legitimate inference that all red noses, *qua* red, are coloured; but from the fact that all good typewriters are silent in operation, it does not follow that a bell is not good unless it is silent in operation. The philosophical move of pointing out that

---

[2]   Cf. *De Veritate*, 2, 9, c.
[3]   Cf. *Summa Theologiae*, 1a, 13, 5 and *De Potentia*, 7,7.

a word is contextually dependent, or 'used analogically', is usually made in order to resolve the difficulties of those who are striving unsuccessfully by other means to avoid making certain inferences. Thus, for example, from the statement that God is good we do not wish to have to make the inference that he possesses certain other qualities inseparably associated with, for example, human goodness. Maimonides (1138–1204) seeks to avoid these inferences by construing 'God is good' as a negative proposition. Alan of Lille (d. 1203) seeks to avoid them by reading it as an assertion that God is the cause of good things. St Thomas replies that we need do no such violence to ordinary language. Since the word 'good' is used *secundum analogiam* (according to analogy), the inference would not in any case be legitimate.[4] The inference does not fail because we are merely punning when we use the word 'good' of God. (Certain things follow concerning a barrel of beer that has been tapped, which do not follow concerning a door that has been tapped, but this is because we are merely punning with the word 'tapped'. Analogical usages, unlike puns, survive translation.) The inferences in the case of language about God fail because 'good' is a contextually dependent word.

There is, however, a deeply rooted superstition amongst certain thinkers that if we are not punning when we use the same predicate of two different subjects, there must be *some* form or characteristic that they have in common. This superstition has resulted in several attempts to 'explain' analogy. For some reason the practitioners in

---

[4]   Cf. *Summa Theologiae*, 1a, 13, 2 and *De Potentia*, 7,5.

this field do not commonly feel called upon to 'explain' univocity. Even the classical Thomist tradition has laid itself open to misunderstanding on this point. The statement that the significata of analogical words are *simpliciter different* (absolutely different) but the same *secundum quid* (in a qualified sense) is perfectly accurate, but it is capable of being misunderstood. It can be and has been read as suggesting that there are two elements in the significatum of analogical words: a principal and important element which is different for each analogical application, and a secondary minimal element which remains the same. And the ingenuity of some philosophers has been exercised in describing this remaining commonness. Analogy is supposed, for example, to involve a 'relation of relations', and so on. From here it is but a short step to treating analogy as a kind of calculation. According, for example, to one author:

We can say that the properties of anything are related to its being in a way proportionate to the relation of the properties of another thing to its being. So:

$$\frac{\text{Properties of created being}}{\text{its being}} :: \frac{\text{Properties of uncreated Being}}{\text{its being}}$$

This does not mean that the properties of uncreated being are related to its existence in a way similar to the relation of the properties of created being to *its* existence; but that as the properties of created being are related to its existence in a manner appropriate to the existence of a created

57

being, so the properties of uncreated being are related to its existence in a manner appropriate to the existence of uncreated being. But we do not know the modalities of the properties of uncreated being; we can only say that it is such as to be appropriate to the existence of uncreated being. But if the analogy of proportionality cannot tell us the modality of the properties of uncreated being, does it in fact tell us anything?[5]

In the above quotation, analogy is viewed as a method of calculating, and a method of calculating which does not work, owing to our ignorance of essential data. We know what goodness is in creatures. The doctrine of analogy tells us that goodness in God is a certain projection of this; only, unfortunately, we do not know the angle of projection. Some philosophers are likely to say that, although, as St Thomas has said, we do not know what God is, nevertheless by analogy we have a certain knowledge of him (a 'non-quidditative' knowledge of God).[6] It is in this context that such writers speak of 'analogical knowledge', 'analogical concepts', 'analogical thinking' and the 'analogy of being'. Yet all this is quite foreign to St Thomas and to the Thomist tradition. For Thomists, analogy is a theory of language concerned with the logical behaviour of certain kinds of words, and more especially with their failure to behave in ways that might be expected of them.

---

[5]   D.M. Emmet, *The Nature of Metaphysical Thinking* (London: Macmillan, 1949), pp. 176–177.

[6]   For a clear criticism of this see Victor White, *God the Unknown* (London: The Harville Press, 1956), Chapter 4.

Goodness, then, is not an essence; it is neither substance, quantity, quality, relation, or any other accident; it is what a Thomist would call a 'transcendental' – in that it transcends the categorisation. Of course the goodness of any particular thing is constituted by substantial and accidental essences: the goodness of a watch is constituted by its accuracy in telling the time, which accuracy, like the watch itself, is a logical construction out of various *entia per se* (beings in themselves). But goodness itself is not a form or nature. It may be asked whether, in view of what has been said about the contextual dependence of 'good', we can speak of *goodness* at all? To this it must be answered that the formation of an abstract noun from an adjective is always legitimate in English, and there is no reason why this linguistic form should mislead us if we are reasonably careful. To protest that there is no such thing as goodness is either to assert, wrongly, that there are no good things, or it is to repeat, less accurately, what has already been said by saying that goodness is a transcendental. In fact, as we shall see, when speaking of God whose essence is not potential with respect to existence, and which therefore does not constitute a limiting context for transcendental words, we can say not merely that God is good but that God is goodness or that goodness is God. In the end, what is common to good things is not that they share a characteristic but that they share a Creator. For St Thomas, to have a concept of goodness in the sense in which we have a concept of redness would be to comprehend God.

Evil as a Real Deprivation

Evil is a lack of good. It is a certain kind of absence. We have seen that goodness is not a property or characteristic of a thing. To attribute goodness to a thing is not to attribute to it the property of being good. Rather, since its goodness consists in its having its own properties, to attribute goodness to a thing is to announce the presence of these properties. Thus to say that people are good is not to say that they possesses the characteristic of goodness; it is to say that they possess certain virtues. To say that they are bad is to announce that some of these virtues are lacking. The word 'evil' signifies what St Thomas calls 'a sort of absence of good'.[7]

St Thomas says '*a sort of* absence of good' (*quaedam absentia boni*), because to say that goodness is absent is not always to say that something is lacking in the properties that make it good. If the goodness of a tree is lacking from my room, this may be merely because there is no tree in my room, and to say this is not to say that anything is evil. There is only a question of evil when the goodness of a tree is lacking from a tree. Absence, explains St Thomas, can be a matter of deprivation or of simple negation:

> The absence of a good, taken simply negatively, is not what is meant by evil; for otherwise it would follow that things that did not exist at all would be evil; or again, that everything is evil because it

---

[7] *Summa Theologiae*, 1a, 48, 1.

lacks the goodness of some other thing; thus, a man would be evil for lack of the speed of a goat or the strength of a lion. But the absence of good, taken as deprivation, is called evil, as the deprivation of sight is called blindness.[8]

The importance, for our study, of the difference between merely accidental characteristics and properties, is that the lack of the former is a mere negative fact about things, whereas the absence of a property is a deprivation, and it is this that is evil.

It is the notion of deprivation that enables us to explain how it is that evil is both an absence and a reality. The general line of explanation can be illustrated by a simple example. An absence of wool is, clearly, simply no wool, and we could not say that a room was full of real no wool. But when the absence of wool takes the form of a hole in a sock, then we are perfectly prepared to say that the hole is real. Similarly, a mere absence of the goodness of a human being (i.e. an absence of the theological and cardinal virtues, etc.) does not constitute an evil until this absence takes the form of an absence *in a human being*.

In what precise sense, then, can we say that a deprivation such as evil is *real*? To answer this St Thomas refers back to the *Metaphysics* of Aristotle.

> As is said in the 5th book of the Metaphysics, 'being' is used in two ways. In one sense it means

---

[8]   *Summa Theologiae*, 1a, 48, 3.

the being of a *thing*; in this sense it is divided by the ten categories, and we can use the word if and only if we can use the word 'thing'. In this sense no deprivation is a being, and hence evil is not a being. In another sense we use 'being' to signify the truth of a proposition which consists in a composition that we indicate by using the word 'is'; this is the sense of 'being' which corresponds to the question 'Is it the case that ...?' It is in this sense that we say that blindness *is* in the eye, or that any other deprivation *is* wherever it is. And it is in this sense that evil is said to be. On account of their ignorance of this distinction, some people, realising that some things are rightly said to *be* bad, and that evil is said *to be* in things, have supposed that evil is a sort of thing itself.[9]

The main point here seems clear enough: evil is real inasmuch as sentences such as 'That man is evil' or 'There is much evil in the history of Poland' can sometimes be used to make true statements. We say that evil is real in order to disagree with those who maintain that evil is nothing, in the sense that it is never really true that anything is bad. Such people try to assimilate the proposition that evil is not a thing to the proposition that the bentness of a stick thrust into water is really nothing. St Thomas's argument is that whereas the proposition that the stick is bent is a misdescription of the state of affairs, and *this* justifies us in saying that the bentness is unreal, the proposition that some man is evil, on the other

---

[9]   *Summa Theologiae*, 1a, 48, 2 ad 2.

hand, is not a misdescription of the state of affairs, and hence we do not have this justification for saying that evil is unreal.

This simple argument is slightly obscured in the minds of some by the notorious difficulties in the passage in the *Metaphysics* to which I just referred. In St Thomas' commentary on this passage[10] he proposes to make three different kinds of distinction:

1 Between *ens secundum se* (a being in virtue of what it is itself) and *ens secundum accidens* (a being according to accident).
2 Between *substantia* (substance) and *accidens* (accident).
3 Between *ens* (being) in either of the latter senses and *ens ... secundum quod significat compositionem propositionis* (the 'being' that signifies the composition of a proposition).

The difficulty is that St Thomas says that distinction (1) 'attenditur secundum quod *aliquid praedicatur de aliquo per se vel per accidens*' (is due to *one thing being predicated of another* either essentially or accidentally); whereas distinction (2) on the other hand is 'secundum quod *aliquid in natura sua* est vel substantia vel accidens' (due to *a thing in its own nature* being either a substance or an accident). At first sight this seems clear enough: distinction (1) has to do with propositions and predication, whereas

[10] *Commentary on the Metaphysics of Aristotle*, Bk V, Lect 9, nn. 885–897.

distinction (2) has not. However, a few lines later he explains that distinction (2) is to be considered *secundum diversum modum praedicandi* (according to a different mode of predication) and he goes on, '*Sciendum est quod praedicatum ad subiectum tripliciter se potest habere*' (It should be noted that a predicate can be referred to a subject in three ways). So it looks as though *both* (1) and (2) have to do with propositions and the composition of predicate and subject, and not simply (1). For this reason it is somewhat bewildering to find a *third* division in which St Thomas proposes to treat of *ens secundum quod 'esse' et 'est' significant compositionem propositionis* (the 'being' according to which 'to be' and 'is' signify the composition of a proposition), as though we had hitherto not been concerned with the composition of propositions at all!

The passage, however, is not so difficult as it seems at first sight. Very briefly, it may be said that for St Thomas all senses of 'being' are basically uses of the *verb* 'to be', and he considers them all in the context of sentences using this verb. The first division he makes has to do with a classification of sentences (what is the relation of the meaning of the predicate to that of the subject?); the second has to do with a classification of the types of statement that can be made with a certain sort of sentence; the third returns to the perfectly general consideration of statements, not now considered according to their categorical type (*modus praedicandi*) but simply considered as true or false. Thus in the statement 'George is an umpire' we can say that 'umpireness' or 'being an umpire' *is*, in the sense that the statement really is true, and it is not a misdescription of any state of affairs to say that George *is* an umpire. But since 'being-an-umpire' is not an *ens secundum se*, but rather an *ens secundum accidens*, and since therefore it does not belong to any of the ten categories, we cannot also say that the 'is' in 'George is an umpire' signifies the being of a thing (*res*). Exactly the same thing can be said of the statement that George is evil. The point that evil is not an *ens secundum se* will recur later when I consider the sense in which evil can be said to have a cause.

We have seen that since evil is a deprivation of good, and since 'good' is a contextually dependent word, whether or not some state of affairs is to be called evil will depend on where, or in what subject, this state of affairs occurs. Lack of speed, as St Thomas said, may be bad for a goat but not necessarily for a human being. This truth must be sharply distinguished from the error that whether or not a thing is bad depends on one's 'point of view'. When a wolf eats a sheep this is good for the wolf and bad for the sheep, but what is in question is not the 'point of view' of the beasts but their *natures*, what they are. Of a very blunt knife I can say either that it is a bad pen-knife or a good paper-knife, and this can really be said to depend upon my point of view, inasmuch as it is for me to decide whether I am going to regard and use this knife as an instrument for sharpening pencils or opening letters. Most of what has already been said in this essay, however, has been devoted to showing that we do not thus arbitrarily determine the natures of things. There are *entia secundum se* such as sheep and wolves, besides *entia secundum accidens* such as pen-knives and paper-knives.

Since evil is a deprivation of good, in order to understand what an evil is we need to know of what good it is the deprivation; and this means that we must know the nature of the thing that is said to be evil. From this it follows that whatever is evil must at least have a nature; it must have its essence, even if all its properties are lacking to it. We can say of evil, as we can say of an accident (though for entirely different reasons), that it cannot be without being in a subject. 'Hence, as every privation is founded in a subject, that is a being, so every evil is founded in some good.'[11] We saw that the essence or substance of a thing is, in a derivative sense, a good. 'It therefore follows that when we consider the initial existence of something as a substance we speak of it as existing without qualification and as being good in a certain respect (namely, inasmuch as it exists).'[12] Thus it is necessarily true that evil always exists in some good. There cannot be anything that is evil without being in some respect good, at least in the sense that it has its first actuality of essence.

It must be recognised, of course, that it is precisely this subject (which must in some respect be good) that is said to be evil: it is the same man who is good, at least inasmuch as he is human, but bad, in so far as he lacks the proper virtues of a human being. St Thomas has two ways of expressing the sense in which a substance, even deprived of its properties, can be said to be good. On the one hand he says that this first act of the thing is *bonum*

---

[11] *Summa Theologiae*, 1a, 17, 4 ad 2. 'Sicut omnis privatio fundatur in subiecto quod est ens ita omne malum fundatur in aliquo bono.'
[12] *Summa Theologiae*, 1a, 6, 4.

... *inquantum est ens* (good insofar as it is a being), and on the other hand he says that the substance is good inasmuch as it is potentially a perfect thing: 'And likewise every potential being, as such, is a good, as having a relation to good. For as it has being in potentiality, so has it goodness in potentiality.'[13] However, it is not difficult to see that these are two ways of saying the same thing, for to say that a subject contains its perfections potentially (and that these are thus potentially real and potentially goods *of the subject*) is the same as to say that the subject is good *inquantum est ens* inasmuch as it constitutes a stage on the way to the realisation of the purpose defined for it by its efficient cause.

The Priority of Nature over Morals

To sum up this preliminary account of evil: it is a deprivation of goodness and, like goodness, it is therefore contextually dependent. Whenever there is talk of evil, we must first be clear about the context in which the evil occurs; we must know, that is, the natures of the things that are said to be evil. Now there have been two significant omissions in this discussion: I have sought to explain the notion of evil without reference either to the positive will of God or to morality. These are significant omissions because they exhibit an order of thought in St Thomas's mind. He differs from some other philosophers and theologians in holding that 'good' and 'bad' are words that we understand and use primarily of natural things. It is in terms of these that we define good

---

[13] *Summa Theologiae*, 1a, 48, 3.

and bad actions, and hence good and bad people: 'We must speak of good and evil in actions as of good and evil in things: because such as everything is, so is the act that it produces.'[14]

Similarly it is this basic use of 'good' and 'bad' for speaking of knives and apples and such things that gives us our foundation for speaking about the goodness of God. In St Thomas's view, we do not know anything about the world through knowing something about God. God is never, for him, an explanation of the world. The movement is always in the other direction: what we know about the world sometimes helps us to know something about God. What we say about the world compels us to make certain statements about God, but no statement about God entails any statement about the world.

It is true that God has revealed to us many things about the world, for example that Mary the mother of Jesus was immaculately conceived; and it is true that this is sometimes spoken of as though we discovered something about the world by deduction from something we know about God as revealing, but this is something of a confusion. When I listen to Fred and he tells me something, my knowledge of what he is talking about is not *deduced* from something I know about him. He is not providing evidence of what he says. He is telling me. Listening to Fred is not the same as examining him or finding out facts about him. When Fred tells me that the

[14]   *Summa Theologiae*, 1a2ae, 18, 1.

house is on fire, I do not argue as follows: 'If Fred says the house is on fire then, because Fred is honest, the house is on fire; but I can hear Fred saying that the house is on fire, therefore the house is on fire.' In coming to know that the house is on fire I *presuppose* that Fred knows what he is talking about, is honest, is not talking in his sleep, and so on; these propositions are not premisses in a deduction. In the same way, when God speaks I listen and do not make deductions or inferences from the behaviour of God. The sin of infidelity consists not in making an error in the deduction, or in wilfully omitting a step in the argument, but in not listening. The case of revelation, therefore, cannot be adduced as a case of finding out something about the world from what we know about God.

One who thinks of God as the explanation of the world has not grasped the absolute transcendence of God; but it is this divine transcendence that is the key to the problem of evil. To this, therefore, I shall turn in the next chapter.

FOUR

The Creator and Evil

Having said something about the nature of good and evil in the world, I must now speak of the relation of the world to its maker. In particular I have to ask whether the presence of evil in the world, understood as I have suggested that we should see it, is compatible with the goodness of God. Our way of talking about God derives from our way of talking about creatures. If we are to talk about God as maker of the world, we must first examine making within the world. In particular, we shall want to know the conditions under which we say that a human being who makes a bad thing is a bad person, and later we shall need to consider whether when we transfer the notion of making to God, these conditions still hold good. My first task, then, will be to make clear what is meant by a good or bad human being and this will involve some explanation of the idea of voluntary activity. Then, having said what moral good and evil are, I shall be in a position to describe the maker or artist in terms of moral value. Thirdly, I shall have to explain the sense in which God is said to be a maker, and say something about the notion of creation. Finally, I shall conclude the argument with a section on the Creator and evil.

Voluntary Activity and the Notion of Moral Evil

So far, I have been concerned with evil as imperfection and defect; I have not yet considered in detail the particular kind of defect that we call moral evil. Moral evil is an imperfection in the operation of the sort of being that has dominion over its operations.[1]

---

[1]   Cf. *Summa Theologiae*, 1a2ae, 1, 1. 'Of actions done by man those

We have seen that the order of finality in causal action extends to the perfection of the thing caused; it does not stop short at the essence shorn of the properties. In the case of some things that are brought into being, the intention of the cause is expressed simply in the nature of the thing caused.[2] St Thomas's favourite example of this is the stone that falls downward: for him this movement is the achievement by the stone of its natural place; it is more perfect when it is near to the centre of the earth than when it is further away. The cause that brings the stone into being (its 'generator') intends that the stone shall be in its natural place, and for this reason the stone by nature moves towards it.[3]

In this way St Thomas distinguishes upward and downward movement of the stone. The former is not natural but must be due to some extrinsic cause acting

alone are properly called "human", which are proper to man as man. Now man differs from irrational animals in this, that he is master of his actions. Wherefore those actions alone are properly called human, of which man is master. Now man is master of his actions through his reason and will; whence, too, the free-will is defined as "the faculty of will and reason".'

[2] Cf. *Summa Theologiae*, 1a2ae, 1, 2: 'An agent does not move except out of intention for an end. For if the agent were not determinate to some particular effect, it would not do one thing rather than another: consequently in order that it produce a determinate effect, it must, of necessity, be determined to some certain one, which has the nature of an end. And just as this determination is effected, in the rational nature, by the "rational appetite", which is called the will; so, in other things, it is caused by their natural inclination, which is called the "natural appetite".'

[3] Cf. St Thomas's *Exposition of Aristotle's Treatise On the Heavens*, Bk II, Lect. 2, n. 305.

upon the stone; but the latter is natural and requires no external cause; its explanation is simply that the stone is this sort of thing. One can only proceed further by asking, 'Why is it this sort of thing?' The answer to this, says St Thomas, is given by referring to the 'generator': the one that brought this stone into being and gave it its nature.

The example is strikingly pre-Newtonian. In classical mechanics it would be ruled out on the ground that the difference between a stone moving upward and downward is merely a matter of the presence in the vicinity of another very large mass, the earth. There are no privileged directions from the stone's point of view. But the question then occurs: What would it be like for stones to be normally *not* in the presence of very large masses such as the earth? St Thomas is, after all, speaking of stones, not of hypothetical particles; and if we isolate the stones from their normal context we thereby deprive them of their 'world', in which their properties have place.

In the case of the stone therefore, the perfected stone, the stone in its natural place, is a purpose for the cause that brought the stone into being; it is not a purpose for the stone itself. It is the purpose *of* the stone within the purposive scheme of its cause, but the stone itself merely acts naturally, deriving its inclination from the purpose of its generator. This natural movement is, however, to be distinguished from any extrinsic movement that the stone might suffer due to the action of some cause other than the one that brought it into being.[4]

---

[4]   Cf. *Exposition of Aristotle's Treatise on the Heavens*, Bk I, Lect. 17, n. 167: 'For we say that a thing suffers compulsion if it is removed

Living things are distinguished from inanimate ones by the fact that it is natural for them to move themselves. The foundation of this difference is that whereas the perfection of, for example, a stone consists of its being in a particular place, a perfection which is achieved by a quite determinate local movement, the perfection of a living thing is of a higher order; that is to say, it is one which could be achieved by one or more of a large number of different local movements. The living thing is not therefore determined by nature to any determinate one of these movements.

I am not, of course, saying that the movements of living things are unpredictable or 'indeterminate' in the modern technical sense of that term, but only that whereas in the case of the inanimate thing there is only one movement which we call natural (the rest being put down to violence), in the case of the living thing, to call one movement natural is not to say that some other movement might not have been equally natural. The difference can be illustrated by considering the different ways in which we speak of a ball rolling down a spiral groove and a rat running through a simple maze towards some food. In the former case we say that the natural downward movement of the ball is impeded by the shape of the groove and that it, therefore, takes on the unusual and unnatural spiralling movement. In the latter case we say that the natural thing for the rat to do, since it

from its proper inclination by the force of a stronger agent. If, therefore, there is not a natural inclination to certain motions in bodies, compulsion has no place in them – any more than blindness would be attributed to an animal if it had no capacity to see.'

naturally seeks the food, is to turn these corners, etc. The rat in the maze, we say, acts just as naturally, given these conditions, as a rat on the open floor; whereas the effect of the impeding groove on the ball is to make it move unnaturally. In other words, the rat can still act naturally in a large number of widely different physical situations, whereas the ball cannot. This may be part of what is meant by the common saying that living things can adapt themselves to their situations. At any rate, the end to which a living thing is determined has to be described in language of a higher logical order than that in which we describe the end to which an inanimate thing is determined.

It should be clear that what I am here doing is analysing the differences between talking of things as animate and talking of them as inanimate. If some investigators choose to describe the rat in the maze in language appropriate to the ball in the groove, they may perhaps be justified for some purposes. In fact, a good deal of interesting work has been done by the 'behaviourists' and others in just this way. My only comment would be that the investigators now in question are no longer regarding the rat as an animate thing.

Clearly, it follows from all this that in the case of any characteristic movement of an animate thing, there can be two descriptions of what takes place. We can, for instance, describe the various local movements of the teeth and tongue of the rat and the food with which these come into contact, and that is one kind of description. To chew and to eat are clearly not two different physical operations. Nor is chewing part of eating in the sense in which chewing is part of chewing and swallowing. To say that a certain action is *chewing* is to describe the movements of the jaws of the animal; to say that this same action is *eating* is to say what function this action has in the whole behaviour and life of the animal. Chewing, we might say, is done by the jaws, but eating is done by the whole animal; eating is a matter of the soul. This is clear from the way in which we would try to answer the question 'Is Fido eating?' when we already see that he is chewing something. All sorts of facts that have nothing particular to do with jaws become relevant to this question: Is he hungry? Is he liking it? etc., etc. In this respect eating is like seeing. If we want to know whether an animal can see or not, we do not examine its eyes, although it sees *with* its eyes; rather, we watch its behaviour; we see whether it behaves in the same way in the dark as in daylight, and so on.

St Thomas calls one of these descriptions a description of the *finis* (end) of what is described by the other description. To say that an animal is eating is not only to say that it is chewing, but also to say that it is chewing for a definite purpose. It is to place the chewing in the context of the animal's purposes. The difference, then, between an inanimate thing, such as a stone, and a living thing, such as a rat, is that while in both cases the movements of the thing are for a purpose, we do not describe the action *of the stone* in the language of movement-for-this-purpose, but simply in the language of movement. We do, on the other hand, describe the action of the living thing in the language of movement-for-this-purpose. We can say that some other cause (whether it be the generator of the stone or not) has a purpose for the stone's action. We cannot say of a stone, as we can of an animal, that it has a purpose for its own action.

To say that an animal has a purpose for its action may sound like the language of fairy tales, but it must be recognised that all that is meant is that the appropriate language for speaking of living creatures involves words like 'seeing', 'watching', 'eating', 'satisfied', 'walking', 'hiding', and 'pursuing', which are all of a higher logical level than the words we use to describe the movements of stones in that there are an indefinite number of such movements that might count as an act, say, of walking. In a parallel way, we say that a word like 'word' is of a higher logical level than a word like 'horse' in that there are a large number of words such as 'horse' that would count as examples of words.

St Thomas summarises what has been said so far as follows:

> The principle of some acts or movements is within the agent, or that which is moved; whereas the principle of some movements or acts is outside. For when a stone is moved upwards, the principle of this movement is outside the stone: whereas when it is moved downward, the principle of this movement is in the stone. Now of those things that are moved by an intrinsic principle, some move themselves, some not. For since every agent

or thing moved, acts or is moved for an end ...
Those are perfectly moved by an intrinsic principle
whose intrinsic principle is one not only of
movement but of movement for an end.[5]

Thus for St Thomas, the movement of a living thing is
more perfectly *its own*, because not only is the movement
an act of the animal but the movement-for-an-end is
also an act of the animal; the purposiveness is not
supplied only by the cause that brought the animal into
being. St Thomas goes on: 'Now in order for a thing to
be done for an end, some knowledge of the end is
necessary.'[6] Here he simply expresses the fact that
purposive and achievement words like 'eating' and
'pursuing' cannot be literally applicable unless awareness
words like 'seeing', 'smelling', and 'startled' are also
literally applicable. The words belong, so to speak, to one
family, and, in fact, it is the appropriateness of this family
of words that determines the genus 'animal'.

So, St Thomas goes on,

whatever acts or is moved by an intrinsic principle
in such a way that it has a certain awareness of the
purpose for which it acts, has in itself a principle of
action not simply that it may act, but also that it
may act for a purpose. That, on the other hand,
which has no awareness of the purpose, even
though it have an interior principle of action, does
not have the principle of action-for-a-purpose

[5]   *Summa Theologiae*, 1a2ae, 6, 1.
[6]   *Summa Theologiae*, 1a2ae, 6, 1.

within itself, but rather another thing has impressed its purpose upon it. Hence that sort of thing is not said to move itself, but rather to be moved by another. But the things that *have* got awareness of their own purposes are said to move themselves ... and therefore, since both their acting and their acting-for-a-purpose comes from an interior principle, their action is said to be 'voluntary'; for the word 'voluntary' implies that the act or motion comes from the thing's own inclination.[7]

This may seem a slightly surprising remark since it is clear that St Thomas includes dogs and rats among the things that have voluntary activity. But for him voluntary activity is correlated with awareness: 'The whole formal character of freedom depends upon the manner of knowing.'[8] It is as true to say that dogs act voluntarily as it is to say that they know the difference between what is food and what is not: 'The voluntary in its perfection belongs to none but the rational nature: whereas the imperfect voluntary is within the competency of even irrational animals.'[9] Voluntary action in the truest sense belongs only to rational beings. The difference between the particular kind of animal that is rational and other animals, from this point of view, is a difference in the awareness that they have of the purpose of their acts.[10]

---

[7] *Summa Theologiae*, 1a2ae, 6, 1.
[8] *De Veritate*, 24, 2. 'Tota ratio libertatis ex modo cognitionis dependet.'
[9] *Summa Theologiae*, 1a2ae, 6, 2.
[10] Cf. *De Veritate*, 24, 1. 'Among those beings which are moved by themselves, the motions of some come from a rational judgment;

The distinction between perfect and imperfect knowledge of the purpose of an act can be stated as follows: perfect knowledge belongs to a being that does not simply know *that which is* the purpose of its activity, but that (a) knows it precisely *as the purpose* of its activity, and (b) knows the sense in which the activity is ordered to it as purpose. In St Thomas's words: 'Perfect knowledge of the end consists in not only apprehending *the thing which is the end*, but also in knowing it *under the aspect of end*, and the relationship of the means to that end.'[11] This sort of knowledge is peculiar to rational beings. Other animals merely apprehend that which is the purpose of their acts.

An extraordinary claim is here being made for rational beings: just as for the stone there is but one action that is natural and to which it is determined, and for the dog there are many actions that are natural in as much as there are several ways of attaining the purpose that is natural to it and to which it is determined, so, for the rational being, there are many *purposes* that are natural to it, for it is not *determined* to anything less than simply being purposive. Just as talk about animal activity involves words of a

those of others, from a natural judgment.' (Eorum autem quae a seipsis moventur, quorundam motus ex iudicio rationis proveniunt, quorundam vero ex iudicio naturali.)

[11] *Summa Theologiae*, 1a2ae, 6, 2. Cf. *De Veritate*, 24, 1. 'Man, judging about his course of action by the power of reason, can also judge about his own decision inasmuch as he knows *the meaning of an end* and of a means to an end, and *the relationship of the one with reference to the other*.' (Homo vero per virtutem rationis iudicans de agendis, potest de suo arbitrio iudicare inquantum cognoscit *rationem finis* et eius quod est ad finem, et *habitudinem et ordinem unius ad alterum*.)

higher logical order than talk about the activity of stones, so talk about rational activity involves yet another level of language – transcendental words such as 'good', 'purposiveness', and 'being'. The perfection of the stone is to be in a particular place; the perfection of the dog is the possession of the particular good proper to its species; the perfection of a human being is 'perfection as such'. We have already seen that 'goodness' or 'perfection as such' is not the name of a property shared by good or perfect things. It is the good of that essence which is not potential with respect to its existence; it is in fact a name of God.

Now the object of the will, i.e. of human being's appetite, is the universal good; just as the object of the intellect is the universal true. Hence it is evident that *nothing can lull a human being's will save the universal good. This is to be found, not in any creature, but in God alone.*[12]

The difference between the stone and the animal is not that the action of the animal is purposive while that of the stone is not, for both of them are purposive. The difference is that, although the action of the stone is purposive, the stone itself is not purposive, whereas the action of the

[12] *Summa Theologiae*, 1a2ae, 2, 8. Cf. *Summa Theologiae*, 1a, 105, 4. 'Now the will can be moved by good as its object, but by God alone sufficiently and efficaciously. For nothing can move a movable thing sufficiently unless the active power of the mover surpasses or at least equals the potentiality of the thing movable. Now the potentiality of the will extends to the universal good; for its object is the universal good; just as the object of the intellect is the universal being. But every created good is some particular good; *God alone is the universal good. Whereas He alone fills the capacity of the will*, and moves it sufficiently as its object.'

animal is purposive with the purposiveness of the animal itself. In the animal, so to say, the stone and its 'generator' are combined in one being. Now in the same way the rational animal combines in one being the stone, the animal, and what gives its purposiveness to the animal. The animal controls and *makes natural* the local motions of the parts of its body, just as the generator makes natural the downward motion of the stone. In the same way, the rational animal *makes natural* the purposive actions of its own body. If the foot of the animal were not part of its body, its only natural movement would be downward, but because it is a part of the organism, its natural movement can be anything that the animal uses to fulfil its purposes, the satisfaction of its appetites, etc. In the same way, if the human body were not part of a human being, its natural activities would be simply those of any other animal, but because it is a part of a human being, the fulfilment of its sensitive appetites is *made natural* by its participation in the specifically human purposes of the human being.

As we have seen, the purpose of the rational being is not determined to anything less than 'purposiveness as such', and just as seeing, hearing, touching, and so on, is the type of cognition correlative to the determinate purposes of a brute animal, so understanding is the type of cognition correlative to the transcendental purposes of a rational being. It is for this reason that understanding, or reason, is the norm of what is *natural* to people. It is natural to a human being to live and act *secundum rationem* (in accordance with reason).[13] This way of considering the levels of being, from stones to people, is like going through a set of

---

[13]   Cf. *Summa Theologiae*, 1a2ae, 18, 5.

Chinese boxes from the inside outwards. The stone, the inmost box, is enclosed within the purposes of its generator. The animal, which is itself purposive, is on the same level as the generator of the stone, and itself contains the parts of its own body; but the animal too is contained within a further box, for it is made with certain determinate purposes. The rational animal is like the third box: it contains the animal which contains the stone. It is some such picture that St Thomas has in mind when he says that the soul of human beings is *in corpore ut continens et non ut contenta* (is in the body as containing it and not as contained by it),[14] and it is this same picture which underlies the ancient notion of the human being as a microcosm of the created universe.

We saw that, for St Thomas, it is characteristic of the living thing that its action is more perfectly *its own* than is the action of an inanimate thing. With the rational animal we arrive at the perfection of this development. The characteristic activity of a rational being is one in which the naturalness of its vital purpose is determined by the creature itself. In the case of a dog we can say that, while the movement of its jaws to the left is not more natural than their movement to the right, the animal is by nature determined to eat and preserve its life. Only corruption and decay or violence can bring it about that the animal does not do this.[15] The movements of the jaws

---

[14]   Cf. *Summa Theologiae*, 1a, 52, 2.
[15]   This is not strictly speaking the case, since individual material things exist for the sake of the whole species; hence the cases in which even healthy and normal animals 'sacrifice' themselves for the good of their offspring, etc.

acquire naturalness by their place in the natural activity of, for example, eating – sometimes this movement will be the natural one, sometimes not. In the case of a human being the naturalness of vital activities like eating and the preservation of life depends in turn on something higher. Sometimes it will be natural to satisfy the appetite for food; sometimes it will be equally natural to starve to death; for 'natural' in this case means 'in accordance with reason' or 'with a view to the *bonum universale*' (universal good), just as the natural movement of the animal's foot meant the movement with a view to eating, etc.

This essay is not the place to examine the moral theory that St Thomas derives from these metaphysical premisses. I have simply been concerned to explain the sense in which it can be said that a rational creature has 'dominion over its acts'. They are its own acts in an absolute sense. The ownership that an animal has over its acts is a genuine ownership, but it exists only within a context determined by the purposes that are previously laid down for the animal by its cause. In the case of human beings there is no such context of limitation.

We are now in a position to explain what moral evil is. Moral evil is a defect in a characteristically human act. That is to say, it is a defect in an act when that act is considered with a view to the *bonum universale* (universal good); it is the defect of not acting in accordance with reason.[16] Any act is evil if it is unnatural; it

---

[16] Cf. *Summa Contra Gentiles*, Bk III, q. 10. 'The conclusion follows, then, that moral fault is found primarily and principally in the act of the will only, and so it is quite reasonable to say, as a result, that

is morally evil if it is unnatural to the kind of creature whose purpose is purposiveness itself.[17] An important point to notice here is that moral good and evil, like any other good and evil, is concerned with the achievement of perfection. A thing is good if it achieves the perfection that is possible and proper to it, and evil if it fails in this achievement. We are speaking, that is to say, of beings that are perfect in virtue of the 'addition' of their proper perfections to their essences. Just as it does not make sense to say that the essence of anything as such is evil, so it will not make sense to say that a being is evil if its perfection is not distinct from its essence. It will be a question, however, whether it is possible in the first place to speak of such a being – whether, that is to say, the notion of *good* is any more applicable in this case than the notion of *evil*.

an act is moral because it is voluntary. Therefore the root and source of moral wrongdoing is to be sought in the act of the will.' (Relinquitur igitur quod morale vitium in solo actu voluntatis primo et principaliter inveniatur; et rationabiliter etiam ex hoc actus moralis dicatur quia voluntarius est. In actu igitur voluntatis quaerenda est radix et origo peccati moralis.)

17 Cf. *De Malo*, I, 4. 'A rational or intellectual nature, in contrast to the nature of other creatures, is related to good and evil in a special way, since nature ordains every other creature for a particular good, and only an intellectual nature by its intellect apprehends the very universal nature of good, and by its appetite of will is moved to seek good in general. And so we in a special way divide evil proper to rational creatures into the evil of moral wrong and the evil of punishment.'

Morality and Making

Before considering this latter question I must say a little about human makers and their artefacts. If people make something that is defective, we may or may not blame them. Under what circumstances do we blame them?

In the first place, what is a defective thing? In order to say that something is defective we have to say what it is. The accusation of making a blunt and hence defective pen-knife can be rebutted by pointing out that what has been made is, in fact, a paper-knife. At first sight this looks as though there need never be any cases of making badly. If I complain that the carpenter has made the chair badly because one leg is shorter than the others, he can always reply that, on the contrary, he has made well a chair-with-one-leg-shorter-than-the-others. To this, of course, the reply is that *qua* carpenter his job is to make *chairs* and in so far as he has failed in this he has carpentered badly. In short, to accuse someone of making badly it is necessary to specify what kind of maker he or she is supposed to be. One cannot be just a *bad maker*; one has to be a bad carpenter or wheelwright or painter. The only badness in virtue of which someone is said to be a bad carpenter is a badness of chairs, etc. Human makers cannot properly be accused of bad making if their products do not serve as effective weapons or reading matter.[18] Thus, in order to be subject to accusations of bad making a human being has to work in a context of demands. Such a person must have a *job*.

---

[18]   Cf. *Summa Contra Gentiles*, Bk III, q.2. 'There is no fault to be found, except in the case of things that are for the sake of an end. A

From what was said in the first section it will be evident that there is, in spite of all this, a sense in which we might speak of people as simply 'bad makers' and not mean that they are bad carpenters or bakers. So long as we place ourselves in the context of beings whose aim it is to make furniture, then a bad one will be one that makes furniture badly. But if we place ourselves in the context of a being whose aim is 'simply to make', then a bad one will be one that simply 'makes badly'.[19] Now it is true of people that the purpose to which they are determined is not any particular one of making this or that kind of thing. They are called good or bad as people not precisely because what they make is good or bad, but because their 'making as such' is good or bad. Thus we distinguish between a good carpenter and a good human being, not as we distinguish between a good carpenter

---

fault is never attributed to an agent, if the failure is related to something that is not the agent's end. Thus, the fault of failing to heal is imputed to the physician, but not to the builder or the grammarian.' (Peccatum non invenitur nisi in his quae sunt propter finem; nec enim imputatur alicui ad peccatum si deficiat ab eo ad quod non est; medico enim imputatur ad peccatum si deficiat a sanando, non autem aedificatori aut grammatico.)

[19] To abstract the act of making from what is made is to speak of *doing* rather than *making*. St Thomas compares the two as follows: 'Yet, if we consider the matter carefully, we shall find the two orders similar from one point of view, and dissimilar from another. There is dissimilarity on this point: moral fault is noticed in action only, and not in any effect that is produced; for the moral virtues are not concerned with making but with doing. The arts are concerned with making, and so it has been said that in their sphere a bad result happens just as it does in nature. Therefore, moral evil is not considered in relation to the matter or form of the effect, but only as a resultant from the agent' (*Summa Contra Gentiles*, Bk III, q. 10).

and a good weaver (who might happen to be the same person), but as between acting according to reason for a particular good, and acting according to reason in general; that is, acting for the *bonum universale*, which includes particular goods within it. Being a human being does not include being a good carpenter in the way in which being a good handyman includes being a good carpenter (as well as being a good painter and plumber); rather, it includes it as a good story about people may include stories about good people but may also include stories about bad people.

Thus, I can sum up my conclusions so far by saying that if a man makes something that is a bad chair, we can blame him as a maker of particular things, if he has the job of carpenter, and not otherwise; and we can blame him as a human being, if being a bad carpenter is contrary to his pursuit of the *bonum universale* (as of course, normally it will be). We have seen that we judge whether or not people are good by those actions of theirs that are characteristically human (just as we judge whether or not an animal is healthy by watching its behaviour towards food, exercises, etc., not by watching it fall off a cliff). Now if a man is a bad carpenter and there is no circumstance that makes it reasonable for him to be so, we may still refrain from concluding that he is a bad man; for it may be that his carpentry does not involve, for him, a characteristically human act. By this, of course, I do not mean that, though it might be, it is not *accompanied* by a characteristically human act; I mean that it does not define the conditions of a human act. The person in question may not perform his carpentry precisely *qua* human being; the action may not be absolutely his own. There will be, no doubt, an act that is his own, but it is not defined by the object 'making a chair', for into that act there have entered other factors which he did not control. In such circumstances we say that he 'could not help' making the chair badly and that therefore his being a bad carpenter ought not to lead us to believe that he is a bad man.

Now we speak of God as the maker of the world; it remains, therefore, to consider how far these considerations about moral goodness and the morality of making are applicable to him and to his world. If his world is defective, are we compelled to blame him or to say that he could not help it?

God as Creator

When we say that God made heaven and earth, what do we mean? In the first place we say that God made heaven and earth 'out of nothing' (*ex nihilo*). It is surprisingly easy to be misled by this, to suppose that somehow it states the difference between what there was before creation and what there is after creation, or even to suppose that it tells us what the universe is made of. Thus in so excellent a work of popular theology as Mr F.J. Sheed's *Theology and Sanity* we find:

> It (the universe) can exist because God, who alone possesses existence as of right, confers existence upon it. God made it. And he made it out of

91

nothing. What else was there for him to make it of? He could not make it of himself, for he is utterly simple and changeless: there are no parts in him which could be subtracted from him and set going as a universe that was not He.[20]

It is true that Mr Sheed soon makes the disclaimer:

We must not misunderstand the statement that God made the universe out of nothing. It does not mean that God used nothing as a kind of material which he proceeded to shape into the universe.

But two pages later he is back with: '... if God having made the universe, left it, the universe would have to rely for its continuance in existence upon the material it was made of: namely nothing.'[21]

This kind of language is appropriate in a work of popularisation, but it could be seriously misleading if taken as theology. What is in question here is not simply a carelessness of language but a metaphysical principle. The tendency to construe *ex nihilo* as in some sense supplying the background to creation is that same tendency, which I have already mentioned, to think of beings as existing in a space of 'not-being'.[22] The fundamental error is not the crude one of supposing that things

---

[20] F.J. Sheed, *Theology and Sanity* (London: Sheed and Ward, 1946), p. 85.

[21] *Theology and Sanity*, p. 87.

[22] St Thomas points out that 'ex nihilo' *can* be taken as referring to the 'background of creation' (*secundo modo importat habitudinem*

are spun out of a material called 'nothingness' but of supposing that creation is the act of supplying the 'vacant inter-stellar spaces' with inhabitants. (It is significant that Mr Sheed remarks in passing, 'When philosophers and theologians ask why anything exists, the alternative they have in mind is nothing.'[23]) A historically interesting variant of this view is that of Newton who thought of absolute space and time as 'the sensorium of God'.

The metaphysical position which gives some substance to this way of looking at things is the doctrine, which I have already noticed, that things can be thought of as being or as not being – creation then being regarded as the passage from the mere possibility of things to their actual existence. This philosophical view I shall call the 'metaphysics of contingency', and it differs radically from the metaphysics of St Thomas. Typical of the metaphysics of contingency is a certain misinterpretation of the *Tertia Via* (the third proof of God's existence) in St Thomas's *Summa Theologiae*[24] (often called the 'Argument from Contingency'), and a tendency to refer to God as the 'Necessary Being'. A brief discussion of this will help to throw light on St Thomas's doctrine of creation.

causae materialis) but only to deny that there is one (*quae negatur*). For a discussion of the use of 'ex' in this context see *Summa Theologiae*, 1a, 45, 1 ad 3.

23 *Theology and Sanity*, p. 84.

24 Cf., for example Mr Sheed's version: 'If we consider the universe we find that everything in it bears this mark, that it does exist but might very well not have existed ... Now it is impossible to conceive of a universe consisting exclusively of contingent beings ... thus we are driven to see that the beings of our experience, the contingent beings,

The basis of the metaphysics of contingency is that what distinguishes creatures from the Creator is their contingency, the fact that they are able not to be. The doctrine is most completely worked out in the metaphysics of Francisco Suárez (1548–1617). *Disputatio* XXVIII of his *Disputationes Metaphysicae* (Metaphysical Disputations) is entitled *De prima divisione entis in infinitum simpliciter, et finitum; et aliis divisionibus quae huic equivalent* (On the first division of being into that which is simply infinite and that which is finite; and on other divisions that are aequivalent to this). This is a division of being between God and creatures, and the second division *quae huic aequivalent* (equivalent to this) is *divisio in necessarium et contingens* (division into the necessary and the contingent).

Clearly on this view, what is not God is contingent. We may immediately contrast this position with that of St Thomas according to which the distinction between necessary and 'possible' (contingent) being is a distinction within the created world. It is the distinction between those beings in which there is composition of matter and form and those in which there is not, between perishable things on the one hand and angels or human souls on the other. Material things are corruptible; they

> could not exist at all unless there is a being which differs from them by possessing existence in its own right. It does not have to receive existence, it simply has existence. It is not contingent but simply is. This is the being that we call God' (*Theology and Sanity*, p. 28). On the contrary, St Thomas calls such a being an angel. Notice that it is included in the universe ('it is impossible to conceive of a universe consisting exclusively,' with the suggestion that it is possible to conceive of a universe that included God), and it *possesses* existence.

are able not to be. Angels are not corruptible; they are not able not to be; they are necessary. But all these things, whether contingent or necessary are distinct from God in that their essences are potential with respect to their existence, whereas in God essence and existence are identical. This distinction between the doctrine of Suárez and that of St Thomas bears upon the account of creation in that for the former, creatures as such are things that *ita non est ut possit esse* (can be or not be) whereas this is not the case for St Thomas. What constitutes creaturehood in his eyes is the distinction of essence and existence.

Unless the distinction between creaturehood and contingency is clearly kept in mind, discussion of God's action in the world can only become muddled. Contingency is due to the distinction of matter and form, and a thing is contingent with respect to the causes to which it owes its form, the secondary causes that brought it into being. Creaturehood is due to the distinction of essence (*essentia*) and existence (*esse*), and a thing is a creature with respect to the cause to which it owes its *esse*, the first cause that created it. All problems concerning the relations between God and creatures, and especially the problem of evil, arise from confusing the action of the first cause with the actions of secondary causes.

Forma dat esse (form furnishes existence),[25] says St Thomas: we account for the existence of a contingent thing by giving its efficient cause, which imposed its

---

[25]   Cf. *Summa Theologiae*, 1a, 42, 1.

substantial form on *materia prima* (prime matter). Such secondary causes really do bring things into existence, but St Thomas asks why *this* is so: why is it true that *forma dat esse*? And his answer is that it is because *this* is a genuine question that we are compelled to say that God exists. For St Thomas, it is not the fact that contingent things exist instead of not existing that demands the action of a creator; this is readily accounted for by their causes – this indeed is why we call them causes. Rather, it is the fact that the existence of contingent beings *is* accounted for by their causes that demands the action of a creator. St Thomas's own arguments for the existence of God are more 'roundabout' than most modern presentations of them. If being is thought of as a sort of form (on the analogy of, say, redness) then just as one can think of a pencil as not having the redness that it in fact has, so one could think of the pencil as not having the existence that it in fact has. And just as one can ask 'Why then does it have this redness rather than not having it?' so one can ask, it seems, 'Why, then, does it have this existence rather than not having it?' But in fact the only sense that can be given to this question is 'Why does it have this substantial form (supposing for the moment that pencils have substantial forms) rather than not having it?' and this question is *completely* answered by saying what brought the pencil into being, its secondary cause(s). Since St Thomas did not think of *esse* as a form but as the *actualitas omnis formae* (actuality of all forms),[26] and since he did not think, therefore,

---

[26] Cf. *Summa Theologiae*, 1a, 4, 1 ad 3. 'Esse est actualitas omnium rerum et etiam ipsarum formarum.'

that one could conceive of a thing precisely as either having or not having existence, on the model of having or not having redness, he has to lead up to *esse* in a roundabout way. God appears in the *Quinque Viae* (the 'Five Ways' in the *Summa Theologiae*) always after a double movement: there are movers, but God accounts for the movers being movers; he accounts for causes being causes, for necessary beings being necessary, for purposes being purposes.

The difference, then, between creation and causality amongst creatures is that a secondary cause operates in a world in which its effect is potential. There are two senses of 'potential' in which a thing is potential before it comes into being: (a) the passive sense in which we say that something is potentially X because it can be made X, and (b) the active sense in which we say that something is of such a nature as to be able to cause X. In both cases the potentiality is there because other things are there. Potentiality is inscribed upon the world.

There is, however a third sense in which we say that something is possible – meaning that it is *thinkable*.[27] In this sense an artefact exists potentially not simply in the efficient and material causes that will bring it into being, but also in the mind of the artist. Artists, *qua* artist, intend to make what they make, and their products can be said to pre-exist potentially in their intention. In the case of the human artist, who does nothing but direct natural causes, such an intention is an intention

---

[27] Cf. *Summa Theologiae*, 1a, 25, 3.

concerning these causes. We cannot intend to work a miracle (though, of course, we can pray for one and even be confident that God will work one), nor can we intend to create. Thus there is no sense in which X is possible in the mind if it is not possible in some efficient and material causes.

Clearly, God intends to make what he makes and so there is a sense in which creatures can be said to pre-exist potentially in his intention. In this sense, there are divine Ideas.[28] Moreover since God's making is not confined to the manipulation of natural causes, as human making is, this possibility in the divine mind does not reduce to possibility in nature, as it does in the case of the human artist. So we must conclude that there is *some* sense in which creatures are possible before they exist and *this* is the sense in which they are potential with respect to *esse*. The important thing is not to confuse this sense of

---

[28] Cf. *Summa Theologiae*, 1a, 15, 1. 'With the exception of what is generated by chance, a form must be the end in the generation of everything. But for agents to act for the sake of a form, the likeness of the form must be in them. This can happen in two ways. In some agents (e.g. those that act by nature) the likeness of the thing to be produced already exists as a natural being: thus people beget people, and fire produces fire. In other agents (i.e. those that act through understanding) the form of the thing to be produced exists as something intelligible – as the form of a yet to be built house exists in the minds of builders. We can call this 'the idea of the house' because builders intend to make houses conforming to forms that they have conceived in their minds. Now since the world is not made by chance, but by God causing through his understanding, God's mind must contain a form to the likeness of which he makes the world. That is what an idea in God's mind amounts to.'

potentiality with the potentiality of a corruptible thing that can, so to speak, be read off it. The fact that such things are generated and corrupted; the fact that we can intend to make them, or imagine ourselves intending to make them or destroy them; the fact (and this is the fundamental thing) that the order of the world is independent of any particular one of them – all this is observable. I do not mean that as such it is an object of the senses (and a phenomenalist would, no doubt, deny that it was observable) but it is matter of experience in such sort that St Thomas can sensibly say, 'Some of the things we encounter are able to be or not to be.'[29] But the fact that each thing is potential with respect to *esse*, that its esse is *received*, is a different matter altogether. In the end, St Thomas's reason for insisting that the essences of created things are potential with respect to existence is that creatures are not God. They are other than God in that, for example, God intends that *they* shall be, whereas, whatever the *complacentia* (delight) that he may be said to have in his own being, he cannot, I think, be said to *intend* that *he* shall be, inasmuch as he does not make himself. But the fact that a creature has only a limited lifetime does not, as such, distinguish it from God;[30] for necessary beings, which do not have a limited lifetime can be distinguished from God. Of course, the

---

[29] *Summa Theologiae*, 1a, 2, 3. 'Invenimus in rebus quaedam quae sunt possibilia esse et non esse.'

[30] The importance of 'lifetime' as a characteristic of material contingent beings is clearly brought out by Aristotle in his *Treatise on the Heavens* 281a.30: 'If there are things capable of both being and not being there must be some definite *maximum time* of their being and not being.'

contingent beings, the things with lifetimes, must be distinct from God, but we have not reached the true *via negativa* (approach by denying) if we simply think of God as other than *them*. In order to reach up towards God we have to deny of him the much 'deeper' potentiality of essence with respect to its act of being.

I was forced to make this brief excursus into the most important and difficult question in metaphysics in order to distinguish creation from what it is not. The result, I hope, is that we can now see that we invoke creation precisely to account for the *esse* of things. Just as the object of every creaturely activity is some form, so the object of God's creative activity is *esse*, which is not a form at all but the actuality of every form.[31]

> But every created agent is limited in its act, as being of a determinate genus and species: and consequently the action of every created agent bears upon some determinate act. Now the determination of every thing in actual existence comes from its form. Consequently, no natural or created agent can act except by changing the form in something; and on this account every change made

[31]   Cf. *Summa Theologiae*, 1a, 45, 5. 'Now among all effects the most universal is being itself: and hence it must be the *proper effect* of the first and most universal cause, and that is God ... Now to produce being absolutely, not as this or that being, belongs to creation.' (Inter omnes autem effectus universalissimum est ipsum esse. Unde oportet quod sit *proprius effectus* primae et universalissimae causae, quae est Deus ... Producere autem esse absolute, non inquantum est hoc vel tale, pertinet ad rationem creationis.)

100

according to nature's laws is a formal change. But God is infinite act ...; hence his action extends to the whole nature of being.[32]

From this it is clear that the act of creation is not an action *upon* anything, since the *esse* of things is what results from creation. Nothing having *esse* can be presupposed to the creative act.

It is tempting here to add 'except, of course, God himself', but this temptation exhibits a failure in understanding. It is no mere verbal quibble to reply that God is *not* a thing that has *esse*. Creation cannot be conceived as what makes the difference between God alone and God with creatures. It would be more accurate to conceive it as what makes the difference between nothing at all and creatures; but since we cannot conceive of 'nothing at all', we cannot really conceive of creation at all. It may seem strange to say that we cannot conceive of X when we seem perfectly capable of using the word 'X'. Surely our being able to use 'X' just *is* having the concept of X, and this is to conceive of X. For the moment, all that I can reply to this is that the concept we have when we use the word 'creation' is, in fact, the concept, or concepts, of *cause*. Now the word 'cause' is itself used analogically; it is contextually dependent like 'good'. To be able to use the word 'cause', therefore, is to be prepared to make the necessary adjustments in each particular context of application. 'Creation' is a word we use when we wish to apply an essentially contextually dependent word without any context.

---

[32] Cf. *Summa Theologiae*, 3a, 75, 4.

Creation is, so to say, that causing which is no particular kind of causing. Now, whereas that colour which is no particular shade of colour is both inconceivable and impossible (because colour is nothing but the genus of particular shades of colour), that cause which is no particular kind of cause is inconceivable but not impossible, because 'cause' is *not* a genus word.

The difference between the 'metaphysics of contingency' and that of St Thomas could be summed up as follows: the former type of philosophy tends to argue that God must exist and must have created the world because it is not conceivable that from *nothing* there should have emerged the existing world. Prior to the world, such a philosopher argues, there must have been not *nothing* but *God*. Against this some philosophers would reply that there is no need for God because it is quite conceivable that the world should have emerged from nothing – why shouldn't it have? Thomists, however, have a third position. They agree that it is quite inconceivable that the world should have emerged from nothing, but they add that this is precisely what happened. They do not feel constrained to postulate God and creation because they find the notion of nothing pre-existing the world repugnant to their minds. On the contrary, in so far as we can picture creation at all we *must* picture it just like this. For the Thomist, God is not invoked to fill a gap left by the absence of anything else. To say that God created the world is in no way to eliminate the intellectual vertigo we feel when we try to think of the beginning of things. Recognition of God's action does not remove any mystery from the world.

The Creator and Evil

In the last section I laid great stress on the difference between the act of God in creating and the action of any secondary cause. As I showed, this difference is due to the fact that, whereas causality within the created world consists in imposing form on matter and has as its object a *form*, creation has as its object *esse*, the actuality of the form itself. In order to talk of creation we have frequently to speak as though *esse* were a sort of form, but this is because *esse* itself is not conceivable. A first consequence of this difference is that the exercise of secondary causality always involves some kind of *change*, whereas in creation there is no change.[33] In the case of an accidental change we have a substance that changes – the water that was once cold becomes hot as the result of some causal action. In the case of substantial change something is *changed into* something else – the hydrogen and oxygen are changed into water. But in creation there is no substance that changes and there is nothing that changes into anything else. *Creation makes no difference* to anything; we could only speak of a difference between existing and not existing if *esse* were a sort of form. The Creator then, is a cause that does not produce any kind of change. From this it follows that certain things *can* be said about the Creator that are said about causes, but certain things *cannot* be said about the Creator which are said about causes precisely in so far as they cause change. It is not, of course, a matter of abstracting the notion of 'sheer causality' from the accidental circumstance of

---

[33] Cf. *Summa Theologiae*, 1a, 45, 2.

causing change, and then applying this purified concept to God. On the contrary, in the case of secondary causes, it is essential to their causality that they cause change. The whole of their causing is nothing but the causing of change; it cannot be separated into two elements, even in thought. We have no purified concept of causality that applies to God in creation; we have simply the word, which, since it is an analogical word, can be used in successive sentences to make statements that, if the word were univocal would be contradictories.

It follows from the fact that creation is not a change that it is not possible to create well or badly, either in the sense that it is possible to *make* something well or badly or in the sense in which it is possible to *do* something well or badly. In the first place, we make something well or badly according to whether what we make satisfies the requirements for making this kind of thing. We make a chair well if we make something that has all that a chair is expected to have. This can mean nothing except in a world in which the chair is potential; it can mean nothing unless the making of the chair takes place in a context. To make is to actualise a potentiality. *To create is to produce the potentiality as well as the actuality*. 'Before' creation there was not only no chair, but there was no possibility of a chair (except in the sense that God eternally intended to *create* the chair and its possibility also) and so nothing can be made of the question 'Does this created thing conform to the requirements for this kind of thing?' Of course, once there is a world we can talk of defective things. We can say that this dog is blind, and that fruit is rotten. But this is just because we are in the context of a world. A blind dog is said to be defective because of the absence of a property (being able to see) and we saw in chapter 2 that properties are only explicable in relation to a world. Thus in creating things God creates also the condition under which it is possible for there to be defect. It follows that we cannot speak of the created thing, precisely as created, being defective. When we say that in relation to God's action no thing is defective, we may seem to be saying that defect is 'really' an illusion, but this is not the case. The fact that things are not temporal in their relation to God but only in relation to each other, does not tend to show that time is an illusion (though, admittedly, some philosophers have thought that it does). To say that things are not defective in their relation to God is not to say that they are perfect or undefective, so that it would be a mistake to regard them as 'really' defective. Rather, it is to say that 'defective' and 'non-defective' are not appropriate words for speaking of the relation of a thing to its creator. This does not make these words inappropriate in their own created sphere.

It is not because God is kindly and loving that he cannot create a defective thing formally speaking (though of course he can and did create a world containing defective things). It is because defect and lack of defect are expressions that can only have application *after* creation. We have already seen (chapter 3) that what is defective must necessarily first be good, but this too is not something we deduce from the character of God; it is something we discover by thinking about the world. As I have said, nothing whatever about the world follows from any statement about what God is in himself.

God, then, cannot create well or badly in the sense of *making* something well or badly. But it remains to show that he cannot do so in the sense of *doing* something well or badly. That is, having shown that he cannot be incompetent (in the sense that creation is not a field either for competence or incompetence) it remains to show that he is not wicked (in the sense that creation is not a field either for wickedness or moral goodness). This will be clear from the considerations advanced in the first section of this chapter. It is blasphemous nonsense to say that God is wicked, but it is equally inappropriate to say that he is morally good. We can say this only in the sense that he is the cause of moral goodness in creatures. Moral good and evil, we saw, belong to rational beings that achieve or fail to achieve perfection. And we saw that this perfection of rational beings could be nothing other than the possession of God, the *bonum universale* (universal good). It follows that there can be no sense in which God can be said to achieve or fail to achieve this perfection, and hence no sense in which he can be said to be morally good or bad.

It is most important to see that this does not mean that we cannot use words of moral praise when speaking of God. We can and must say that he is loving, kind, compassionate, just, righteous, and provident, and when we say this we use words that signify moral goodness in their application to human beings. They signify moral goodness, however, because of the created context in which they are applied. When we apply them to God, however, we use them without such a context. When we say that God is compassionate we mean that goodness which occurs in us as the moral virtue of compassion belongs to God without the restricted particularity that it has in us.

> We know God from the perfections that flow from him to creatures, and these perfections certainly exist in him in a more excellent way than they do in them. Yet we understand such perfections as we find them in creatures, and as we understand them, so we use words to speak of them. Thus we have to consider two things in the words we use to attribute perfections to God: first, the perfections themselves that are signified (goodness, life, and the like); second, the way in which they are signified. As far as the perfections signified are concerned, we use the words literally of God, and in fact more appropriately than we use them of creatures, for these perfections belong primarily to God and only secondarily to other things.[34]

---

[34] *Summa Theologiae*, 1a, 13, 3. 'Deum cognoscimus ex perfectionibus procedentibus in creaturis ab ipso; quae quidem perfectiones in Deo sunt secundum eminentiorem modum quam in creaturis. Intellectus autem noster eo modo apprehendit eas, secundum quod sunt in creaturis: et secundum quod apprehendit ita significat per nomina. In nominibus igitur quae Deo attribuimus est duo considerare, scilicet perfectiones ipsas significatas, ut bonitatem, vitam et huiusmodi; et modum significandi. Quantum igitur ad id quod significant huiusmodi nomina, proprie competunt Deo, et magis proprie quam ipsis creaturis, et per prius dicuntur de eo. Quantum vero ad modum significandi, non proprie dicuntur de Deo: habent enim modum significandi qui creaturis competit.'

It is, of course, only possible to apply *literally* to God those words of moral praise that do not contain contextual limitation as *part of what they signify*. Thus, while one can say that God is *just* quite literally, even though one only knows justice as something occurring in created beings, one cannot literally call God temperate, because a thing cannot be temperate if it does not have sensual appetites. Nevertheless one can say metaphorically with the psalmist: 'Yahweh is compassionate and gracious/ Slow to anger and rich in kindness.'[35] To have said this (that it makes no sense to speak of God as competent or incompetent, as morally good or morally evil) is already to have answered the 'problem of evil', which is formulated on the assumption that such talk makes sense. It remains to apply this conclusion in various fields. We must see in what senses God can be said to be the cause of evil and in particular we must deal with a closely related problem about freedom and divine causality.

---

[35]   Psalm 103:8.

FIVE

The Cause of Evil

In the previous chapter I aimed to show the implications of the transcendence of God. We have seen that the formulation of the problem of evil with which I began is a typical metaphysical muddle. That is to say, it contains phrases that seem to make familiar sense but that on examination turn out to be senseless because they employ words outside their proper context. The problem of evil is stated by asking questions about God that can only intelligibly be asked about creatures. It derives its apparent force not from its intelligibility but from the exigencies of the imaginative picture that we inevitably have of God and the world. When someone asks 'Is God omnipotent or is he good – which do you choose?' there is something unsatisfying about the reply that the question cannot arise about God since no sense can be made of the suggestion that he might be incapable or defective. The questioner hankers after an explanation that will show *how* God is both good and omnipotent. The questioner wants to be able to see the world with its defects no longer as the product of an evil or incapable being, but as made by a good and omnipotent God.

There is a sense in which this request must be refused and another sense in which it can be acceded to. Just as we saw that the doctrine of creation does not remove any of the intellectual vertigo that people may feel when they contemplate the coming to be of the world out of nothing at all, so my remarks upon the problem of evil will not remove any of the vertigo we feel when we contemplate the world of pain and misery entirely in the power of an infinitely good and powerful God. Just as the 'metaphysics of contingency' strives to remove the mystery from creation, so various attempts have been made to remove the mystery from evil (some of these attempts were dealt with in chapter 1). There is, however, a sense in which someone may rightly demand to 'see' the world with its defects and sins as the work of a good and omnipotent God, but what is in question here is the kind of seeing that faith brings and, finally, the kind of seeing that beatitude is. Through the supernatural strength of faith we are able to learn from God's revelation about his divine plan for the world, and we are able in a certain sense to say 'Yes, of course!' But all this is something we are only able to do when we have seen clearly the metaphysical errors involved in the first formulation of the problem of evil. In this chapter I shall be concerned to apply what I have previously said about the transcendence of God to two particular questions that naturally arise in connection with this discussion. They are: 'What, then, causes evil?' and 'How is this transcendent power of God compatible with human freedom?' This chapter will not exhibit any new metaphysical or theological notions that have not already been discussed, but I hope that by applying the notions already expounded I shall make them a bit clearer.

The Cause of Evil

To ask what is the cause of evil, in the language of St Thomas, would be to ask four different possible questions, for, like Aristotle, he distinguished material, formal, final and efficient causality. That is to say, he distinguished four different kinds of questions that our *admiratio* (wonder) might elicit in our minds. But, as he himself points out, two of these questions (concerning formal and final causality) do not arise in the case of evil, which is a privation of form and of due finality. Evil is, so to say, precisely recognised by the inapplicability of these questions. We have, then, to ask 'In what do we find evil?' and 'What brings it about that questions of formal and final causality are thus inapplicable?' In other words, we have to ask about the material and efficient causes of evil. Evil as we have already seen, must necessarily be subjected in good. Nothing can be sheerly evil, since a privation must be a privation of and in something. This suffices to answer our question about the material cause of evil. The more complicated question concerns the efficient cause of evil, and it is with this that I am immediately concerned.

St Thomas asserts that evil has not got a cause *per se* but only *per accidens*. This is not a way of saying how evil has got a cause. It is a way of saying how evil has *not* got a cause. It is a way of explaining how it is that we speak as though evil as such is caused when it is not. St Thomas usually distinguishes between *per se* and *per accidens* in this sense by means of an illustration from sensation. Colours are *per se* visible, sounds are *per se* audible, but if you hear a bell that happens to be blue, you might say, 'It was the *blue* one I heard.' It might thus be necessary to point out that blueness is only audible *per accidens*. This does not mean that blueness is, in a certain sense, audible; it means that it is not audible at all, but someone might possibly be misled into thinking it was audible by the form of the language. The distinction enables us to differentiate the functions of the adjectives in 'I heard the blue bell' and 'I heard the clanging bell,' since clanging is *per se* audible. It is because it clangs that the bell is audible at all, whereas its being blue has nothing to do with its audibility. In the same way, when we say that evil has a cause *per accidens* we do not mean that it partly has a cause, or that it has an indirect cause; we mean that *as such* it has no cause but that we speak as though it had one. It is because we have names for evils that we talk like this: we speak of the cause of an illness or of blindness, or we speak of someone being responsible for a sin. Indeed, if it is the case, as I suggested earlier in this essay, that the notion of cause first arises by contrast with what comes about naturally, evils and defects and distortions will be the first things we associate with causes. Nevertheless we ask 'What is the cause?' in order to find out in what way the puzzling thing is, after all, natural. To ask why someone is in the unnatural state of blindness, is to ask what natural effects of other things (germs or other causes) have produced this state in that person. When we ask for the cause of an evil, we reply by giving the cause of some good things that happen to be evil for this other thing. We do not give a cause of the evil as such. Thus, just as the thing we hear *happens to be* blue, so the good thing that is caused *happens to be* evil for some subject, and it is in this sense that we can speak of a cause of evil. It is a perfection and a good of a fire to heat, but if what it is heating is an animal, this very heat may be an evil for the animal. It is not here a question of 'points of view'. The heat really is bad for the animal just as it really is good for the fire, but it is caused as a good and perfection of the fire.

St Thomas distinguishes two ways in which a cause can produce an effect that happens to be an evil. In the first place, the cause itself may be defective in its action. It is clearly *per accidens* to the causality of a thing that the thing is defective, and in such a case we have a further question: how is it that the cause is defective in its action? In the second place, an action can produce an evil *per accidens* because the production of something good involves the perishing of something else that is good. All change involves evil in this sense, since in all change a form is gained only at the expense of another which is lost. This is true both of accidental change and substantial change, though the considerations advanced in the last chapter show that it is not true of creation, which is not a change.

The first way in which evil can be produced *per accidens* sometimes reduces to the second way and sometimes not. When an agent is defective in its action because of some defect in its own generation or because of some violence it has received (as when I paint badly because I have injured my hand, or because I was born colour-blind), then this defect reduces to a *per accidens* defect brought about by the perfection of something else. This is not the case, however, with an agent that is neither defective in its generation nor suffers violence, and such is the case with people in so far as they are intellectual creatures, and with angels. Our souls are not generated but created, and hence they cannot suffer any defect for which they are not themselves responsible. We shall see more of this later.

The second way in which evil is produced *per accidens* is a condition of what St Thomas would call the sublunary material world. The qualification 'sublunary' is necessary in order to do justice to his thought, because he regarded the celestial bodies as material and yet ingenerable and incorruptible. It may not be so simple as it might at first appear to excise this doctrine from his cosmological theory, for much of what he has to say about time and place depends upon it. It is possible that much of what St Thomas wished to say about the superlunary world has been transposed by modern cosmology into talk about the subatomic sphere. This, however, is a speculation that cannot be developed here. For the moment, I will speak only of the material world of corruption and generation. In such a world it is *inevitable* that generation should be accompanied by corruption and that things should have lifetimes at the end of which they corrupt. This is not a condition of a *created* world as such, but of a contingent world. If this did not happen, we should not say that the world was contingent and material. There is nothing in the distinction of essence and existence, which marks the creature as such, to necessitate such a state of affairs. A creation consisting simply of angels, for example, or one in which the only material things were 'celestial bodies', would not be subject to this kind of evil. Given, however, that we have a material world that is a field of *becoming*, then the coming to be of one thing, and its continued existence, depend upon the perishing of other things. When we breathe, oxygen perishes.

It is not, therefore, an evil for the world as a whole that there should be evils for particular things in the world.

On the contrary, given that it is a material world, it is a necessary and good thing that things should happen that, *per accidens*, are evils. It cannot intelligibly be argued that it is an evil thing to have a material world at all because of the evils that this entails for particular individual things, for if the world were not material there would be no particular individual things.

We have seen that God intends the good of the whole world. This is no more than to say that there *is* a good for the whole world, for we have seen that the notion of 'the world' is not prior to that of God. We can only speak of a whole world, as distinct from speaking of this thing and that thing, because we speak of God. It is for this reason that, since God made the world to be material, and since he intends the good of this material world, we can say that he is the cause of this kind of evil *per accidens*. It is not weakness that prevents him from making a material world in which there is no corruption, but the logical impossibility of an incorruptible contingent world.

So far, I have been concerned with what St Thomas calls *malum poenae* (evil *suffered* by things).[1] We have seen that evil *done* by things because of a defect in the action of the cause can, in the case of things that are simply produced by substantial change, be reduced to *malum poenae* in the causes producing them. But a rather different problem arises in the case of defects in the action of beings that are not thus within the order of the

[1]   Cf. *De Malo* 1, 4 and *Summa Theologiae*, 1a, 48, 5.

material world. Evil that results *per accidens* from defect in the action of a being that is not produced by another creature, but that is directly created, i.e. a rational being, is called by St Thomas *malum culpae* (evil of fault, or blameworthy evil). Of course there is a sense in which people are produced by substantial change, and in this sense they can inherit defects of action, but they cannot inherit defects that they themselves will,[2] and it is the evil which *per accidens* results from the acts of their will that St Thomas calls *malum culpae*.

Evil and Free Will

I shall be concerned in this section exclusively with *malum culpae*, the moral evil that we do. In the first place, like any other deprivation it has no *per se* cause. It is caused *per accidens* in the willing of something good. Every turning away from the *bonum universale* is consequent upon a turning towards a *bonum particulare* (particular good) that is inconsistent with it. The especial interest of this form of evil for us is that in this case the causality is not reducible to the cause that intends the whole world.

Aquinas puts this point by saying:

> God is the author of the evil of pain, but not of the evil of fault. And this is because the evil of pain

---

2 It might be thought that the doctrine of original sin is some sort of exception to this, but such is not St Thomas's view. He points out that although original sin is in each person born of Adam, it is not voluntary by the will of each person. Cf. *Summa Theologiae*, 1a2ae, 81, 1.

takes away the creature's good ... But the evil of fault is properly opposed to uncreated good; for it is opposed to the fulfilment of the divine will, and to divine love, whereby the divine good is loved for itself, and not only as shared by the creature.[3]

The opposition here is not between the created goods of this life, which are lost by *malum poenae*, and the uncreated good of the next life, which is lost by *malum culpae*, for in St Thomas's view beatitude is a *bonum creatum* (created good) – the vision of God is not itself God. Neither, however, is it an opposition between the evil that is a defect in creatures and an evil that is a defect in God, for there cannot be any defect in God; he cannot be harmed by anything. Indeed, a little later St Thomas explicitly denies that any evil is in this sense opposed to the uncreated good. He writes: 'Since evil is privation of good ... it is opposed to that good which has some potentiality, but not to the supreme good, who is pure act.'[4] The opposition is between two goods considered as objects for human desire: one is a created thing that participates in the divine goodness; the other is the *bonum universale*, the uncreated good itself.

---

3   *Summa* Theologiae, 1a, 48, 6. 'Deus est auctor mali poenae, non autem mali culpae. Cuius bratio est, quia malum poenae privat bonum creaturae ... malum vero culpae opponitur proprie ipsi bono increato: contrariatur enim impletioni divinae voluntatis, et divino amori quo bonum divinum in seipso amatur: et non solum secundum quod participatur a creatura.'

4   *Summa* Theologiae, 1a, 49, 3 ad 2. 'Cum malum sit privatio boni ... illi bono opponitur cui adiungitur potentia: non autem summo bono, quod est actus purus.'

Someone may lose the former in *malum poenae*; a person turns from the latter in *malum culpae*.

It is in this clarification that we have the clue to all the problems to which our free will gives rise. Freedom, in the sense of freedom of choice, is sometimes thought of as a capacity of ours to stand over against God. All other material creatures, it is thought, are absolutely determined in their action; they do exactly what God decrees that they shall do. But God has left us free to choose for ourselves. We escape from the determinism of the material world. It is argued that if this were not so there would be no such thing as acting against God, of offending him or disobeying his command. This position is succinctly expressed in a remark from the Talmud: 'All is in the hands of heaven except the fear of heaven.'[5]

All virtue as well as all vice would be an illusion, so some say, unless we were free over against God. The exponents of this argument are divided into those who conclude that freedom is a kind of illusion and those who hold that people are in some sense independent of God's causality. The latter sometimes hold that while God foreknows what someone will do, nevertheless he does not cause it.

St Thomas takes up neither of these positions, for he questions the argument upon which both are based. His solution is set out lucidly and succinctly in a beautiful passage in his *Commentary on Aristotle's 'Perihermeneias'*.

---

[5]   Ber. 33 b.

God knows with certainty and infallibly all that is to come to pass in time. Nevertheless those things that happen in time are not thereby necessitated in their being or in their coming to be ... The divine will itself is the source both of necessity and contingency in things; it is the source of the proximate causes of things, upon which depend the necessity or contingency of the effect. For an effect that he wishes to occur necessarily, God provides necessary causes, while for an effect that he wishes to occur contingently, he provides contingent agents. And according to these different kinds of causes, effects are called either necessary or contingent, although all of them depend upon the divine will.[6]

St Thomas deals directly with the effect of this on the theory of morals. He brings up the following objection to the view that God moves even our free will:

If God moves the will, it follows that voluntary actions are not imputed to us for reward or blame. But this is false. Therefore God does not move the will.[7]

His reply is to deny the implication. What makes our acts free, and therefore meritorious or wicked, is not the fact

---

6   *Commentary on Aristotle's Perihermeneias*, Bk I, Lect. 14, n. 197.
7   *Summa Theologiae*, 1a, 105, 4 obj. 3. 'Si igitur Deus moveat voluntatem, sequitur quod opera voluntaria non imputentur homini ad meritum vel demeritum. Hoc autem est falsum. Non igitur Deus movet voluntatem.'

that they are *not* caused by another, but the fact that they *are* caused by us:

> If the will were so moved by another as in no way to be moved from within itself, the act of the will would not be imputed for reward or blame. But since its being moved by another does not prevent its being moved from within itself ... it does not thereby forfeit the motive for merit or demerit.[8]

The difficulty arises because it is not easy to see how a human act can be caused by something other than the person in question and yet also be caused by that person, and this is difficult because we forget that the *other* in this case is God, who transcends the created world.[9]

Within creation an act is due in its entirety either to A or to B. It is true that A may be using B as an instrument or that A may be a 'higher level' cause than B (as we saw in chapter 2), but in such a case we distinguish the causality.

---

[8]   *Summa Theologiae*, 1a, 105, 4 ad 3.
[9]   Cf. *De Veritate*, 24, 1 ad 3. 'God works in each agent, and in accord with that agent's manner of acting, just as the first cause operates in the operation of a secondary cause, since the secondary cause cannot become active except by the power of the first cause. By the fact, then, that God is a cause working in the hearts of men, human minds are not kept from being the cause of their own motions themselves. Hence the note of freedom is not taken away.' (Deus operatur in unoquoque agente etiam secundum modum illius agentis; sicut causa prima operatur in operatione causae secundae, cum secunda causa non possit in actum procedere nisi per virtutem causae primae. Unde per hoc quod Deus est causa operans in cordibus hominum, non excluditur quin ipsae humanae mentes sint causae suorum motuum unde non tollitur ratio libertatis.)

We saw, for example, that precisely as a thing of a certain shape, certain materials, etc., a paintbrush simply transfers paint from palette to canvas, but precisely as an instrument, by its instrumental causality, it paints a picture. It is not this, however, that is in question here. It is not by instrumental causality that people are the cause of their own acts; it is by their own natural causality. It is possible to characterise creation by saying that the Creator's instruments have their instrumental causality in their own right, as their nature. No creature can create or be a means of creation because no creature can make something whose whole nature is to be the creature's instrument. I can channel and guide natural forces; I can bring it about that they should occur here rather than there, and with these others, and now rather than then. In this way I can make artificial things that are my instruments, but I cannot make an *ens per se* whose 'to be' is to be my instrument. In my instruments there is a distinction between the thing and the function I have for it. It is only God who has instruments in which 'to be his instrument' is the same as 'to be', whose works are characterised simply by the fact of received *esse* and nothing else.

For St Thomas, then, the distinction between beings that are free and beings that are not is a distinction within creation; it does not have to do with whether or not they are entirely dependent upon God. That this is true is evident from the way in which we in fact decide whether a creature is free or not.[10] What we ask is not whether its

---

[10] Cf. *De Veritate*, 24, 1 ad 2. 'No one would say that people do not have free choice merely because they cannot will or choose in the manner in which God or an angel can.' (Nullus autem diceret,

act was determined by God or not, but whether it was determined by some other creature.

Whatever, then, is *per se* caused by any creature, whether it be free or not, is caused by God inasmuch as he is the cause of whatever has *esse*. Besides this we may say that God is the cause of certain effects that result *per accidens* from the *per se* causality of some creatures, inasmuch as he created the kind of world in which such effects follow *per accidens*, and which requires such effects for its perfection. Thus, to have created a world of material things with lifetimes is to have created a world in which corruption is the *per accidens* effect of generation, and in this sense God is the cause of such corruption.

We cannot, however, in either of these senses say that God is the cause of the kind of *per accidens* effect of people that we call sin. He is not its cause in the first sense, since sin is a deprivation and has no *esse*, and only comes about *per accidens*;[11] but neither is he its cause in the second sense, since God has not created the kind of world in which sin is *required* for the perfection of the whole. Deprivation can only be needed for perfection in a world of forms that can only be the acts of matter, a world, in fact, of things with lifetimes. In the world of non-material beings there is no *place* for deprivation at all. It is for this reason that whereas the frustration of a

---

 propter hoc hominem non esse liberi arbitrii, quia non potest taliter velle vel eligere qualiter Deus vel angelus.)

[11] Cf. *De Potentia*, 3, 6 ad 1. 'Malum ... cum non sit ens, sed defectus entis, non potest esse, per se loquendo, factum.'

purely material thing, in virtue of which it fails to attain its end, may be only relatively an evil (its frustration may be required for the fulfilment of the whole pattern), the frustration of an immaterial thing, such that it fails to attain its purpose, is absolutely speaking an evil; there is no context in which it is good. Thus, while we may say that the punishment of hell is good and is something that is caused by God, we cannot say that there is any sense in which the sin that is punished in hell is good or is caused by God. The doctrine that God makes us good in order to bring us to heaven is one thing, but the heresy that he makes us sin in order that we shall go to hell is senseless.

What then can we say of sin and the causality of God? We can say first of all that, while God could not have created a world of things with lifetimes that was of its nature incorruptible (though he might miraculously sustain such things and prevent their corruption, as will be the case with us after the resurrection), he could have created a world without sin. This is implied by my assertion that sin plays no part in the perfection of anything. We are then tempted to say that if God could have made a world without sin but did not do so, he is responsible for the sin. We may grant that this does not remove the responsibility from the sinners, but we might still want to attach it to God – just as when we say that social conditions are responsible for crime we are not saying that criminals are not sinners but that those responsible for the social conditions are sinners too. But here we must remember what I said in chapter 4. Although God could certainly prevent sin from occurring without any interference with human freedom, he does not *do* an evil when he permits evil to happen. St Thomas brings forward the objection that to do evil and not to do evil are contradictory opposites. In the case of such opposites the denial of one entails the assertion of the other, and hence, the objector argues, since God does not wish evil *not* to be done (as is clear from the fact that evil *is* done, for God's will is never frustrated) he must wish evil to be done. In reply St Thomas points out that, although *to do evil* and its negation *not to do evil* are contradictory opposites, it is not the case that 'X wishes evil to be done' is the contradictory opposite of 'X wishes evil not to be done' since, as he says, both are affirmations.[12] Hence the denial of the latter (i.e. the denial that God *wishes evil not to be done*) does not entail the affirmation of the former (that God *wishes evil to be done*). All that such a denial entails is that God does *not wish evil not to be done* and this is called 'permitting' evil. We may pursue this analysis a little further and point out that since evil is a privation of some good *evil not done* is the same as good done; although, since good is *not* a privation of evil, *good not done* is *not* evil done. We may therefore translate 'God does not wish evil not to be done' as 'God does not wish a certain good to be done' and, as has been said, this is not the same as

---

[12] Cf. *Summa Theologiae*, 1a, 19, 9 ad 3. '"Evils exist" and "Evils do not exist" are contradictory statements. But '"God wills evils to exist" and "God wills evils not to exist" are not so opposed since each is affirmative. God neither wills evils to be nor wills them not to be. He wills to allow them to happen, and this is good.' (Licet mala fieri, et mala non fieri, contradictorie opponuntur; tamen velle mala fieri, et velle mala non fieri non opponuntur contradictorie, cum utrumque sit affirmativum. Deus igitur neque vult mala fieri, neque vult mala non fieri: sed vult permittere mala fieri. Et hoc est bonum.)

to wish that evil should be done. Simply not to wish that there should be a certain good is in no sense evil. If God had created four more sparrows than in fact he created, he would have done, and willed to have done, a certain good, but it was not evil to refrain from willing that this good should be done.

For creatures such as us, what we do not will and what we do not do can be as morally significant as what we do will and do. To fail to do what one ought to do is as wicked as to do what one ought not to do. But this is precisely because we exist in a moral context in which we ought to do this rather than that. We are born with a nature that determines what it shall be good for us to do and what evil. But, as I have tried to show throughout this essay, there is no such context for God. God is not any kind of thing. There is nothing that it is natural for God to do, and nothing unnatural. He cannot have duties or a way of life. He has no function and no place in any order. All creatures are *his* and hence are ordered towards him. And he is not *his*. Before he does anything there is no reason for doing it rather than not doing it. There is not even a 'before'. He does not have good reasons for what He does. Rather, he *is* the reason for what he does.

Conclusion

This essay has been fundamentally concerned with the transcendence of almighty God. The argument has taken place over what is called the problem of evil and I have shown that there is no inconsistency in asserting that the infinitely good God created this world in which there is evil and sin. I have not done so in such a way that the reader who is convinced by the argument can say 'Now it is clear to me why there is evil in the world; now I have the explanation.' Just as the *Quinque Viae* do not, in my opinion, seek to explain how the world came into being by invoking God, so St Thomas's account of evil, which I have outlined, does not seek to explain the evil in the world. When we speak of God we do not clear up a puzzle; we draw attention to a mystery.

There was however a puzzle, and it has been cleared up above in the way that metaphysical puzzles are usually cleared up: by showing that the formulation of the puzzle depends upon the use of words outside their proper context. But the theological value of my discussion must lie in the fact that the context in question embraces the whole created world. I have not been dealing simply with words that have a particular limited context and are properly used only in connection with some class or genus of things. To limit the range of application of such words and to show how puzzles arise from their improper use is one important philosophical task. But I have been concerned not with such words but with language that seems to have application to absolutely any being, and I have been asking about *its* limits of applicability.

I have been asking, in fact, about the limits of language itself. I have been saying to objectors that they have been trying to push words not simply beyond the boundaries of their particular fields but beyond beings altogether. I grant them that their dilemma would hold good if God were a being amongst beings, however great and powerful and loving he were; that is, their dilemma would hold if God *had* existence. If the problem could be stated that way, it would be insoluble. But I have tried to show more than that the problem cannot be stated *that way*: what I have constantly tried to show is that God is beyond the world in which it can be stated. In the second and third chapters I have tried to show how certain metaphysical terms are used within the world, and in the fourth and fifth chapters I showed how to speak of God is to speak of what is beyond the world – to speak of that towards which our words can reach out, but which cannot be enclosed within our words.

There remains no better way of expressing this fundamental truth of the transcendence of God than the traditional one: that God is his *esse*, whereas the *esse* of creatures is received. Creatures do not *differ* from God. God is not what is left over when you remove creatures. God and creatures cannot be thought of together, or even apart. It is simply that what is not Him is His.

AFTERWORD

A Personal Memory

It is fitting that what may turn out to be the last of Herbert McCabe's published works is also his earliest. Herbert worried away at the same fundamental theological issues throughout his life: What is evil and how is it reconcilable with the goodness of God? What does it mean to be free? How are faith and reason related? In what sense is a consecrated host the body of Christ? And so on. His asking of questions like these was an integral part of his discipleship of Jesus.

In a brilliant sermon delivered in 1982 he argued that St Thomas's particular form of sanctity was to grapple with the most basic question of all, to accept the question as an important one, and then to be defeated by it: What is God? People are saints not because of what they achieve but because of their acceptance of failure, which they hand over to God, just as Jesus had to confront the failure of his mission and hand it over to the Father on the cross. In Herbert's own words, Thomas's sanctity of mind

> was shown not in the many questions he marvellously, excitingly answered, but in the one where he failed, the question he did not and could not answer, and refused to pretend to answer. As Jesus saw that to refuse the defeat of the cross would be to betray his whole mission, all that he was sent for, so Thomas knew that to refuse to accept defeat about this one question would be to betray all that he had to do, his mission. And this question was the very one he started with, the one he asked as a child: What is God?[1]

---

[1] *God Still Matters*, p. 236.

This was Herbert's path to sanctity too. That was why he returned constantly to the same questions not so that they could be solved and thus disposed of, but because all that intellectually rigorous work brought one closer to the mystery beyond the reach of our words. He wrote: 'Our language does not encompass but simply strains towards the mystery that we encounter in Christ ... The theologian uses a word by stretching it to breaking point, and it is precisely as it breaks that the communication, if any is achieved.'[2]

A computer would have been perfect for Herbert's way of working. It would have allowed him to go over texts time and time again, polishing, honing, finding a clearer way to express his thoughts. I tried several times to persuade him to use one, but he stubbornly refused, since he loved his ancient Olivetti portable typewriter. One day, to his horror, it was stolen from his room. That day he happened to be on the rota to hear confessions at Blackfriars Priory in Oxford, and the story has it that someone confessed to theft. Herbert gave the penitent the task of finding his typewriter and, it is said, it was there by the confessional door before the end of the session! One of the reasons that he published so little in his life – he has been much more productive since he died, with the help of his brother Brian Davies OP – is because every lecture was just a step on the journey, provisional, as far as he had got so far.

Herbert rejoiced in debate but could become very irritated if one failed to defend one's position intelli-

[2] *God Still Matters*, p. 177.

gently. When he was preparing his brilliant little catechism (originally published in 1985) he sent out drafts to a large number of friends, asking for their reactions and corrections. I was in a bit of a rush at that time, but, to show willing, I jotted down a few points and hoped that to be the end of it. Herbert, however, summoned me to his room to drink wine and justify my comments. And he would not let me go until agreement had been reached on every issue.

Although he was perhaps the best preacher I have ever heard, he was always nervous beforehand. This was not stage fright so much as a profound sense of the responsibility of the preacher to proclaim the gospel as intelligently and engagingly as possible. In the sacristy at Blackfriars, Oxford, and before the concelebrants processed in to celebrate the Eucharist, he would often tell us that he had nothing to say and that surely there was someone else who could preach instead of him. Preaching, for Herbert, was not a game. Although his sermons often sounded spontaneous, every one was written and rewritten before he delivered them. He was once asked to teach young friars the art of preaching. The trouble was that he could never bring himself to really criticise their efforts, since he knew too well how frightening it is to have to open one's mouth at all.

Herbert could be a difficult and crotchety man. 'Sanctity' might not be the first word that springs to mind when remembering him as someone to live with. But he detested pretention and glib cleverness. A poor deacon who engaged in over-elaborate liturgical choreography was shocked by Herbert's oaths when he bent for a blessing before reading the gospel. Herbert had strong views, which he would defend aggressively, not only on theology but on most things, from how to wash dishes to Irish politics. When I first met him he was initially rather frosty, assuming that someone from my privileged background must be an enemy of the working class, from which he sometimes gave the impression of coming, middle class though he was! But he was also capable of immense sensitivity and kindness. If he ever hurt anyone, he was always deeply repentant.

As a young friar I was once asked to take part in a television debate on Gnosticism. I was so excited at the prospect of being on the screen that I temporarily overlooked the fact that I knew nothing about the subject. This became evident during the programme, which was broadcast live. I flew back from Manchester to Heathrow feeling ashamed and deeply regretting my stupidity for ever having accepted my invitation to speak. When I got back to Blackfriars in the early hours I found under my door a note from Herbert saying how wonderful I had been and how proud he was of me. I knew that it was not true, but I have always kept that little note as an expression of Herbert's profound, fraternal kindness.

Besides his preaching, I miss above all his exuberant enjoyment of life, his festivity, his desire to celebrate. One quickly learnt that his invitation to go out for 'a quick half' of beer was not to be taken literally. I doubt whether he ever drank a half pint in his life. He once described the life of the Trinity in terms of a conversation in a pub:

> Think for a moment of a group of three or four intelligent adults relaxing together in one of those conversations that have really taken off. They are being witty and responding quickly to each other – what in Ireland they call 'the Crack'. Serious ideas may be at issue, but no one is being serious. Nobody is being pompous or solemn (nobody is preaching). There are flights of fancy. There are jokes and puns and irony and mimicry and disrespect and self-parody. Now a 7-year old is in the room, completely baffled by it all … Now this child is like us when we hear about the Trinity.[3]

I am sure that Herbert will now have entered that conversation and be filled with the joy of it.

---

[3] *God, Christ and Us*, p. 115.

APPENDIX 1

Categories

Some people hold that there is only one kind of genuine statement which can properly be said to be true or false. They say that apparent statements which are not of this kind are in fact not statements but persuasive utterances intended not to convey truth but to encourage the listener to adopt a particular attitude or policy in living; among such pseudo-statements are usually included ethical and theological doctrines. I think that these people are mistaken but it is not my purpose here to vindicate the statement-making character of ethical and theological language. What I propose to argue is that there are not one but many different types of statement. By this I do not simply mean that there are many different types of sentence or many different ways of formulating truths, but that the word 'statement' has to be used in several irreducibly different senses and cannot be treated as a univocal term. This I take to be Aristotle's and St Thomas' theory of the Categories. If this theory is correct the way is at least open to an intellectualist ethics and theology; it will at any rate not be possible to say that because a statement is not a factual one it is neither true nor false.

1. Meaning and Grammatical Function

People often say nowadays that the meaning of a word is the way in which it is used. When they say this they are usually concerned to reject the naive opinion that the meaning of a word is something that the word stands for, that, as Professor Ryle has put it, every word is related to something which is its meaning in the way that the name Fido' is related to the dog Fido.[1] Wittgenstein characterises such a naive theory as follows: The individual words in a language name objects–sentences are combinations of such names. In this picture of language we find the roots of the following idea: Every word has a meaning. The meaning is correlated with the word. It is the object for which the word stands.'[2] In this essay I am taking it for granted that such a view is inadequate. What I want to do is to examine the alternative opinion that the meaning of a word is given by giving the rules for its use.

I think there is an important difference between explaining to a foreigner the difference in English between 'horse' and 'pony' on the one hand and between 'horse' and 'froid' on the other. Doubtless in both cases we would be explaining rules of the English language but there would be such different kinds of rules involved that this general account of what we had been doing would not be very helpful. When all is said and done there remains some sense in saying that Peter's French grammar is quite good but his vocabulary is not very large. Doubtless in increasing his French vocabulary Peter will be learning rules of the French language but not the same sort of rules as he learned when he was acquiring his grammatical skill.

Any artificial formalisation of a living language is rightly suspect nowadays, but for the sake of clarity I am going

---

[1] Review of Carnap's *Meaning and Necessity in Philosophy*, Jan. 1949.
[2] *Philosophical Investigations* (Oxford, 1953), Part I, 1.

to codify the distinction I have referred to by distinguishing between the grammatical function of a word and its meaning. What grammarians used to call 'Parts of Speech' is a rough classification of words according to their grammatical functions. I shall say that two words have different grammatical functions when a well-formed expression containing one of the words ceases to be a well-formed expression when the other word is substituted for the first. Thus, for example, 'The table laughed heartily' remains a well-formed expression if we substitute 'chair' for 'table' but not if we substitute 'therefore' for 'table'. Thus in this case at least 'table' and 'therefore' have different grammatical functions.

I want to suggest that we do not normally inquire about the difference in *meaning* between two words unless they have the same grammatical function. Generally speaking learning the *meaning* of words is a matter of extending your vocabulary and not of mastering your grammar. In some of its common uses the word 'to' differs in meaning from the word 'towards', but we would not, I think, normally say that there was a difference in *meaning* between 'towards' and 'federation'. Similarly 'rarely', 'often', 'sometimes', 'not' and 'almost' can form a group with one grammatical function within which there are differences of meaning and so can 'cabbage', 'antelope', 'sky-scraper' and 'postman'; but the differences of meaning in one group are of a quite different sort from those in the other, and the difference between a word in one group and a word in the other is only a difference of meaning in a very extended and artificial sense of that word.

One of the reasons why we say that there is a difference in meaning between 'bread' and 'Jana' but are reluctant to say that there is a difference in meaning between 'bread' and 'because' is that in English we speak not only of the meaning of words but also of the meaning of sentences. The use of 'meaning' as applied to sentences is closely related to its use as applied in a restricted way to words of one grammatical function, but not so closely related to its use as applied indiscriminately. If I have a sentence with a certain meaning and I change one of its words for another word of different meaning but with the same grammatical function, I shall get a new sentence which will either have a new meaning or, perhaps, will be a piece of nonsense, but if I change one of its words for a word of different grammatical function I shall not have a sentence at all. Thus if I start with 'The boy was playing with a piece of string,' I can substitute for 'boy' a word of the same grammatical function but different meaning. As a result I may get, for example, 'The kitten was playing with a piece of string' (which has a new meaning) or perhaps 'The window was playing with a piece of string' (which is nonsense but is still a perfectly good sentence). But if I substitute a word which differs not merely in meaning but in grammatical function, too, for example 'occasionally', I shall get 'The occasionally was playing with a piece of string' (which is not just nonsense, it is not a sentence at all).

It is most important to recognise that there is a great difference between an expression which is a sentence but nonsense and one which is not a sentence at all. In the first place nonsense sentences can be and are used as part of the

144

language, we use them for telling fairy stories, for example. In the second place we can give reasons why a nonsense sentence does not make sense – 'Windows can't play with string' – but very often we cannot give a reason why a string of words does not make sense; there is no reason why it should.

To avoid confusion I shall henceforth not speak of sentences as meaningful or unmeaningful, I shall instead say that they make sense (are sensible) or do not make sense (are nonsense); I shall keep the word 'meaning' for words and phrases and I shall not speak of a difference in meaning between words or phrases of different grammatical functions. I shall use the word 'expression' for any word or group of words. A sentence is an expression that is well-formed in accordance with the grammar of the language. Just as a sentence is an expression in which the constituent expressions are rightly ordered in accordance with their grammatical functions, so a sensible sentence is one in which the constituent expressions are rightly ordered in accordance with their meanings. We can sometimes criticise malformed expressions with remarks like 'It hasn't got a main verb'; we criticise nonsense sentences with remarks like 'Walruses can't really talk.'

I am now going to examine the relationship between the sense of indicative sentences and the meaning of the expressions which function as subjects in these sentences. This is, of course, but one small problem out of many similar ones but I choose it for special consideration firstly because it is interesting in itself and secondly because it involves questions that philosophers in Europe have been thinking about for a very long time. If we cannot be right in a small matter where we have the successes and failures of a long tradition to learn from, there is no point in pontificating in general terms about Meaning and Truth.

2. Criteria of Nonsense. (a) The Principle of Verification

It will be well to begin by noting the difference between the general view I am taking of sense *versus* nonsense and the view, which used to be common amongst some logical positivists, that the sense of a proposition is the way of showing whether it is true or false. According to this Principle of Verification a sentence makes sense if it expresses a true or false proposition; otherwise it does not make sense. In opposition to this doctrine I am taking the view which is fairly common amongst contemporary philosophers that the question of whether or not a sentence makes sense is a question about the ordering of its constituent expressions in accordance with their meaning, and has nothing to do with truth and falsity. I think that the logical positivists were mistaken in supposing that truth or falsity attached to something called a 'proposition' which a sentence expresses. The word 'proposition' is useful for expressing the relationship between different languages, as when we say that 'Je me trouve à Paris' in French expresses the same proposition as does 'I am in Paris' in English, but it simply will not do to say that the proposition expressed by 'I am in Paris' is true or false any more than one can say that the sentence expressing it is true or false. The quite unmysterious reason for this is that when I am in Paris I may use the French or English sentence which expresses this proposition and will thus say something that is true, but when I am not in Paris I may use exactly the same sentence expressing exactly the same proposition and thus say something that is false. Truth and falsity belong not to propositions or sentences as such but to particular uses of sentences. One can no more describe a sentence or proposition by saying that it is true than one can describe a pair of shoes by saying that George wore them on Tuesday; certainly if he wore them they would at least be a pair that would fit him and this would characterise them to some extent, but they would fit him whether he wore them or not. Just as a pair of shoes can be black size nines with rubber soles even in a country where nobody ever wears shoes, so a sentence can make sense even at a time or in a place in which there is no occasion when it is used for saying something true or false. To take the classical example, 'The present king of France is wise' makes perfect sense even though today it cannot be used for saying anything true or false because there is no king of France to talk about truly or falsely. The sense of the sentence is exactly the same as it was in the seventeenth century when there was a king of France; it retains this sense even though nowadays there is no way of showing that what it expresses is true or false.[3]

---

[3] This point is made very clearly by Mr Strawson ('On Referring', *Mind*, no. 235, July 1950, p. 320). From this article and from his *Introduction to* Logical Theory (London, 1952) I have borrowed the terminology of 'Referring' and 'Statement'. My general indebtedness to Mr Strawson's writings will be obvious though I hasten to absolve him of any responsibility for the theory of Substance that I am putting forward.

3. Criteria of Nonsense. (b) Appropriateness – The Predicables

It seems clear, then, that when we ask whether 'The king of France is wise' makes sense, we are *not* asking whether the proposition it expresses can be verified; I want to suggest as an alternative to this view that one of the things we *are* asking is whether the meanings of the subject 'The king of France' and of the predicate '… is wise' are such that they are appropriate to each other. We are asking, among other things, whether the sentence is or is not like 'The king of France is an exact multiple of three' or 'The breadknife was snoring unusually loudly' in which the predicate is not appropriate to the subject.

The notion of the appropriateness of a predicate to a subject is not a simple one, for there are many ways in which predicates can be appropriate. Professor Ryle has recently protested rightly against the 'undiscriminating employment of smother-expressions like "Quality", "Property", "Predicate", "Attribute", "Characteristic" …' to cover anything which is said about a thing.'[4] He attributes this to the hold which Aristotelian logic had upon seventeenth and eighteenth-century thinkers among others. This is scarcely fair to the Aristotelian tradition

---

[4] *Dilemmas* (Cambridge, 1954), p. 85. This is perhaps a suitable point to note that Professor Ryle's use of 'Category' (e.g. *ibid.*, p. 9 and in the phrase 'category mistake', *The Concept of Mind*, p. 16, etc.) seems to me quite different from the Aristotelian usage. Broadly speaking his categories have to do with different types of words in sentences whereas Aristotle's categories have to do, as I shall suggest, with the distinction of types of statements.

which in fact contained a definite, if rudimentary, theory of the different ways in which a predicate can function. The Aristotelians distinguished five different things that can be covered by the smother-expression 'Predicate'; these were called the five *Predicabilia or Universalia* and they were: *Genus, Differentia, Definitio, Proprium,* and *Accidens.* These five represent five different ways in which a predicate can be appropriate to a subject, five ways, that is, in which an indicative sentence can make sense. It seems unlikely that this can stand as an exhaustive or final treatment of appropriateness, but I propose to work for the moment within this traditional framework since there seem to be no modern developments of the theory. (I think that the simple bipartite division, which used to be fashionable, into factual and tautological propositions represents a crude retrogression rather than a development of the Aristotelian theory.)

It is difficult to define precisely the sense of each of the five predicables without first seeing their relation to each other, so I propose to begin with a fairly vague account of the predicable of *Accidens.* For a scholastic philosopher the first temptation to be resisted is that of confusing the predicable *Accidens* with the predicamental or categorical *Accidens.* The categories, as we shall see, are not a classification of predicates in their relation to subjects; they have nothing to do directly with the ways in which *sentences* make sense; they are a classification of certain types of true or false *statements* that sensible sentences can be used to make. The statement that a certain (categorical) accident belongs to a substance may often be made by means of a sentence in which the predicate is appropriate to the subject not as a (predicable) accident but, for example, as a *proprium*. For example, 'George can think' and 'George is pink' are sentences in which the predicates are appropriate to the subject in different ways, that is, they make sense in different ways, but both may be used for attributing an accident (in the categorical sense) to George. Conversely 'George is happy' and 'George is on my left' are the same from the point of view of the predicables but the statements they can be used to make are categorically different. To ask, as scholastics sometimes do, whether such and such is a predicable or a categorical accident is to muddle up two different kinds of question; it is like asking, 'Does the Equator pass through Kenya, or is it merely a geographical fiction?'

In order to avoid this sort of confusion I shall not use the word 'accident' in the sense of predicable accident. Instead I shall call a sentence in which the predicate is appropriate to the subject in the way peculiar to a predicable accident a 'factual sentence'. I shall keep the word 'accident' for use in connection with the distinction of different types of statement. Any introduction of technical vocabulary necessarily produces a distortion of everyday speech, and it is worthwhile drawing attention to some of the distortions that have been produced here. Notice in the first place that '"p" is a factual sentence' is not equivalent to '"p" is a fact' or to 'It is a fact that p.' I am simply going to rule out sentences like '"p" is a fact' because they would be hopelessly misleading. As for 'It is a fact that p,' I shall interpret this as saying two things: (a) that 'p' is a factual sentence, and (b) that the sentence is being used to make a true statement. Thus a statement made by a sentence of the form 'It is a fact that p' would be false if either 'p' were not a factual sentence or the statement that 'p' was used to make were false. Thus the statements made by 'It is a fact that God exists' and by 'It is a fact that London is smaller than Wigan' will both be false, but for different reasons, the latter because London is bigger than Wigan and the former because 'God exists' is not a factual sentence. 'God exists' is not a factual sentence because the way in which '… exists' is appropriate to 'God' is not the way in which the predicate of a factual sentence is appropriate to its subject.

After these preliminaries we are in a position to give some account of what a factual sentence is. First of all I want to explain by examples the term 'contrary predicate'. The predicates '… doesn't hunt beetles in the cellar' and ' … is rather tall for his age' are the contrary predicates respectively of the predicates '… hunts beetles in the cellar' and '… is not taller than average for his age.' I can only explain this fairly simple notion by means of examples because a living language is too fluid to be governed by rigid rules for the formation of contrary predicates. All that can be said as a general rule is that in the case of a predicate P, the contrary predicate of P is one which when attached to a subject yields a sentence which could be used to make a statement by which we would deny the statement made by the sentence in which P is attached to the same subject. We can then say, as a first approximation, that a sentence is a factual sentence when the predicate is appropriate to the subject in such a way that the contrary predicate would be equally appropriate. Thus sentences such as 'I came here on Tuesday,' 'My kangaroo is hungry,' 'Peter bought a new car,' 'The litmus has turned red,' are factual sentences and the corresponding sentences with contrary predicates – 'I did not come here on Tuesday,' 'My kangaroo is not hungry,' etc. – are also factual sentences. In such sentences the meaning of the subject is in no sense a reason for preferring any predicate to its contrary and if a factual sentence makes sense with a certain predicate it will necessarily make sense with the contrary predicate.

4. The Meaning of the Subject and Restriction of the Predicate Range

I now want to suggest that there is an important sense in which the meaning of a word which functions grammatically as the subject of an indicative sentence is given by giving the types of predicates (and their contraries) that can be attached to it to yield factual sentences that make sense. It is because of the meaning of 'window' that we think there is something odd about the question, 'Was the window playing with a piece of string?' The question looks like the question, 'Was the kitten playing with a piece of string?' but we recognize that the answer 'No' would not have the same force in the two cases. We think that the question about the window is a bit like the catch question, 'Have you stopped cheating at poker?' which carries with it the perhaps unjustified presupposition that you have been cheating in the past. The question about the window seems in the same way to carry with it the unjustified presupposition that the window might have been playing with string. But this is not peculiar to the question about the window, for the question about the kitten carries with it the same sort of presupposition but in this case we do not notice it because it is justified and it does not seem queer. I am not suggesting that all questions are like 'Have you stopped cheating at poker?' For that question is peculiar in that it presupposes a *fact* about you, the fact, namely, that you have been cheating at poker, whereas what is common to all questions is that they presuppose not an extra *fact* but that the sentence expressing the act makes sense. They presuppose, that is to say, that the meaning of the subject is such that the predicate in question and its contrary (a question offers a choice between the two) fall within the restricted range of predicates that can sensibly be attached to the subject.

It is clear that some subjects such as 'My black pencil' will exercise two sorts of restriction over the range of predicates that can be attached to them. It is one sort of restriction that excludes both the predicates '… is not hungry' and '… is hungry,' and another sort that excludes '… is not black' but does not exclude '… is black.' The reason why '… is not black' is inappropriate is that in calling something 'My black pencil' you have already begged the question about its blackness, you have incorporated into your naming a presupposition of fact about the pencil which is incompatible with its not being black. A question about a black pencil already presupposes a *fact* (much as the question 'Have you stopped cheating at poker?' presupposes a fact) as well as presupposing a certain predicate range within which the answer must fall. Thus in learning the meaning of 'My black pencil' you are learning not merely a rule but also certain particular exceptions to the rule. In accordance with the first sort of restriction you learn that to the subject in question you may not sensibly attach any predicates other than '... is P' and '... is not Q,' '... is G' and '... is not Q,' '... is R' and '... is not R,' etc. In accordance with the second sort of restriction you learn that you may not attach '... is not Q.'

5. Rules of Meaning that Have no Exceptions – Definable Words

The next step in this theory that the meaning of a subject expression is given by giving an account of the predicates that can appropriately be attached to it, is to examine the possibility that we might have subject expressions which, unlike 'My black pencil', exercise only the first sort of restriction over their predicate range. To learn the meaning of such expressions would be to learn rules of appropriateness to which there were no particular exceptions. I want to suggest that we might use as names expressions which do not incorporate any presuppositions of fact about what they are naming. To illustrate what I mean I shall take the classical example of the noun-phrase 'human being'. The meaning of this expression I shall take to be given purely and simply by giving the types of predicate that can be attached to it. This is part of what is meant by the Aristotelian who says that it is possible to *define* a human being and who goes on to say that a human being is a rational animal. To say that a human being is an animal is not, for the Aristotelian, to state any facts about human beings or to describe human beings in any way; it is to say that it makes sense to speak of human beings as hungry or not hungry, as trying to climb on the table or not so trying, as in pain or not in pain, as being young or growing old. Similarly to say that a human being is rational is not to say that human beings are understanding anything or thinking about anything; it is to say that it makes sense to say of them that they are guilty or not guilty, seeing or failing to see the point of an argument, making or not making decisions, clever or stupid, unscrupulous or charitable. When Whitehead emended the traditional definition to 'Man is an animal intermittently liable to fits of rationality,' he was saying not less but more than the Aristotelian says. As far as his definition goes the Aristotelian is not claiming that any human being can think or is liable to think, but only that it would not be nonsensical to say that he has been thinking. Of course, as Aristotle is at pains to point out[5] having said that a human being is a rational animal there remains a great deal more to be said. There remains the investigation of what is involved in being a rational animal. We have to discover empirically just what is the logical behaviour of the predicates authorised by the definition; we have to find out how we use words like 'sees', 'feels', 'hungers', 'wants' and 'dislikes'. The definition at first roughly circumscribes what I think Wittgenstein would call a 'language game'. It remains for us to discover in detail how it is played. In learning the internal economy of the game we become more precise about its boundaries and we may well find that our original definition needs to be modified or understood in a new way. It is important to recognise, however, that since a definition is not a collection of facts or a description, no empirical discoveries can make it logically necessary to modify our definition.

---

[5]   *De Anima*, 1.1, 402b, 15 *et. seq.*

Nevertheless we do modify our definitions and we do regard some language games as better than others. Part of the theory of substance is an attempt to explain what we are saying when we say this. There is nothing to prevent us from deciding arbitrarily upon a language in which such and such factual sentences will make sense and such and such others will not. Thus, for example, Malebranche decided that 'My dog is in pain' did not make sense (and used to beat his dog every day to proclaim his faith in this). His position was not that 'My dog is in pain' always makes a false statement because 'My dog is not in pain' always makes a true one but that both these sentences are nonsensical like 'My telephone is in pain' or 'My dog is in mortal sin' or 'My dog is not in mortal sin.' Clearly, if we happen to disagree with Malebranche we cannot simply adduce facts to discredit him since the argument turns precisely on what is to count as a factual sentence; nevertheless most people do think that his definition of a dog is an incorrect one because they do want to be able to say that dogs are in pain or not in pain. This is the sort of case that St Thomas is thinking of when he says:

> Si quis ergo assignet definitionem per quam non deveniatur in cognitionem accidentium rei definitae, illa definitio non est realis sed remota et dialectica.[6]

The position that I am going to maintain is that to assert concerning something that its essence has such and such a definition is to assert something that claims to be true.

[6] *Comm. in De Anima*, Lect. i, n. 15. ('If a definition is given which will not lead to a knowledge of the accidents of the thing defined, this is no real definition but an abstract and dialectical one.')

But for the moment we must return to the meaning of 'human being'.

As has been said, when an Aristotelian says that a human being is an animal he is not asserting that a human being has certain characteristics or that he is recognisable in this or that way, but only that it makes sense to assert or deny that he has these characteristics or ways of being recognised. 'George is an animal' might, though I think misleadingly, be described as a second order predication as compared with 'George is hungry.' 'George is an animal' gives a reason why 'George is hungry' and 'George is not hungry' make sense. It establishes a language game in which these sentences have a part to play. It is not a factual sentence and its predicate cannot be synonymous with or the contrary of any predicate in a factual sentence whose subject is 'George'. When we say that it is a fact that George is hungry, we are not expressing but *making use of* our knowledge that George is an animal. That George is an animal is not part of what is asserted or denied by the statement that he is hungry. If we say that George is hungry and so George must be an animal we are making use of an odd kind of implication which is quite unlike the kind we make use of when we say that George is free, white and twenty-one and so he must be white; it is more like saying that this piece has put the king in check so it must be a chessman.

'George is an animal' makes sense in a different way from a factual sentence: the latter makes sense if the predicate does not fall outside the range of predicates in factual sentences authorised by the meaning of the subject term, the former states (partially) what the meaning of the subject term is. In traditional terminology the predicate 'is an animal' is predicated in 'eo quod quid'; the predication belongs in the predicable of *genus* and not of *accidens*. The sentence may be used for stating *what* the thing referred to by the subject is. Among the five predicables three are of this kind. The Aristotelian tradition distinguishes the ways in which 'George is an animal,' 'George is rational' and 'George is a rational animal' make sense, and these three ways are respectively the predicables of *genus, differentia*, and *definitio* (the latter is sometimes misleadingly called '*species*'). For the present it must suffice to say that the difference between these three is that a sentence in which the predicate is appropriate to the subject as a *definitio* completely circumscribes the meaning of the subject, while the other two do so only partially and their ways of being partial are quite distinct. All three, however, yield sentences which can be used to say *what something is*, rather than what it is like or what has happened to it or what it has done or will do, etc. I have not discussed and shall not be able to discuss the predicable of *proprium* although it is of great importance in the Aristotelian theory. It has to do with complications which can, I think, for the moment be ignored.

6. The 'Facts about the World or Else Rules of Language' Theory

At this point, if not a good deal earlier, the reader will have come to suspect that all I am doing is making rather heavy weather over a simple distinction that has become almost a platitude among contemporary philosophers: the distinction between facts about things and rules of language. A great many people would admit that there is an important distinction between sentences like 'George is an animal' and sentences like 'George is hungry,' and they would make the distinction as follows. 'George is hungry' can be used to state a fact about George, whereas 'George is an animal,' although it looks as if it could be used to talk about George, is in fact used to talk about the word 'George'. It is used to say that the word 'George' has such a meaning that a certain range of predicates such as '... is hungry' or '... is not ill' can be attached to it to make sense. Such people would say that 'George is hungry' is used to state a fact about the world, while 'George is an animal' is used to state a rule of language, and some of them would call the latter sentence a 'tautology' and would prefer to say that it is used to express or show a rule of language than to say that it is used to state such a rule. These people would point out that the truth or falsity of the statement made by 'George is hungry' depends upon some contingent events in the world, so that we *cannot* say that it is true or false without examining the world around us empirically, whereas the truth or falsity of the statement (if any) made by 'George is an animal' depends not on any contingent events in the world but on the constitution of the language which we have constructed to talk about the world. These people frequently say that sentences like 'George is an animal' cannot be used to convey information about the world. Sometimes they regard such sentences as expressing an attitude or a policy towards George on the part of the man using the sentence.

This is a very simplified account of a set of opinions which is fairly common among contemporary philosophers and I want to agree with a great deal of what these people say. I think that one of the things that they want to insist on is that if you are simply telling someone about the meaning of a word you are not giving him the kind of information you would be giving him if you told him that there was a horse in the bathroom. I think this is clearly true. But the view does seem to rest on the assumption that since when you assert that 'George is an animal' you are not stating a fact about the world, then you must be stating or expressing nothing but a rule of language. This I find unsatisfactory. In the first place I cannot see that there are any facts about the world. I do not see that any obvious sense can be given to the statement that a sentence such as 'The water has come to the boil' can be used to make a statement about, or state a fact about, *the world*. To me it seems that it is used to state something about some water, and that it can be so used because first of all it makes sense; and it makes sense because 'The water' has a meaning such that '… has come to the boil' can be appropriately attached to it. I do not know what the meaning of 'The world' is, or (what is the same thing) how we could decide what it makes sense, or does not make sense, to say about it. Of course 'The world' has a perfectly ordinary meaning when we distinguish it from e.g. 'The sun' or 'The stars' or 'Europe', but clearly this is not what these philosophers mean by it when they say that some sentences can make statements about the world. In the second place I think that if you say that 'George is an animal' is a tautology you may be overlooking what I think is an important difference between the sense in which 'The old grey mare is old' is a tautology and the sense in which 'George is an animal' is a tautology, but I shall not discuss this point at present.

I think that underlying a great deal of what some people say about facts and tautologies, or what some people used to say about what were called 'truths of fact' and 'truths of reason' is the unexamined presupposition that there exist side by side a World full of things or decorated with facts, and a Language full of words or decorated with sentences, and that part of the philosopher's job is to sort out what belongs to the World and what belongs to Language. It is a little like what the Aristotelians used to accuse the Platonists of believing in, an extra world governed by logic and meaning set over against the ordinary world with no government to speak of. In such a set up explaining the meaning of a word is like explaining the proper moves of a pawn in chess without explaining that people play chess and try to win. It is possible to do this but there is always the danger that the learner will come across the word 'winning' and ask what sort of move is a winning move. (Just as a man might ask: What sort of a sentence is a true sentence? What sort of a name is a proper name? or What sort of a description is a definite description?) The teacher will then patiently explain that a winning move is not a sort of move and that he cannot explain what winning is in the terms in which he has been explaining the game. The learner is then liable to ask why the teacher has restricted himself to this way of explaining the game, and whether there might not be more to be said about moving a pawn than an account of the rules according to which it is moved. Not that in explaining the rules one can say more in the sense of telling the learner that on some occasion Capablanca moved his pawn to a particular square, but that in explaining them one is also in some sense explaining why people move pawns at all. In a rather similar way when we say that George is an animal we may sometimes be doing more than giving the rules for the use of 'George', not in the sense of telling anybody any particular facts about George but rather in the sense of pointing out that statements of fact can be made about George, that there is, so to speak, some point in having sensible sentences with 'George' as subject.

In other words one cannot complete the job of describing a Language and then pause, turn round to look at the World and add some additional information about the correspondence between the two. Rather the world permeates all of one's definitions of some parts of language, some definitions are worldly definitions. One does not say in the first place that 'chair' is used in such and such a way and then add as a further fact that it names something in the world (what in the world is *something*?). Some of one's definitions are like explanations of the moves of chess, in which the whole explanation is permeated by and presupposes the notion of playing the game and trying to win, but others, like the explanation of 'chimera' are like explanations of the rules of a game which nobody plays or wins or enjoys. There is not much point in having a set of sensible sentences beginning 'The chimera is …' because nobody will ever want to use these to make true or false statements, for there are not any chimeras to make statements about. It is the latter type of explanation rather than the former that needs to be accounted for on the face of it, and the contrast between the two induces us to try to explain what makes a game a real game, just as the contrast between what we do when we define 'chimera' and what we do when we define 'human being' leads us to talk about being. The only difference seems to be that there are human beings but no chimeras. As St Thomas says:

Si non sit aliqua res cuius essentiam definitio significet *nihil differt* definitio a ratione exponente significationem alicuius nominis.[7]

---

[7] Comm. in 11. *Post. Anal.* Cap. VII, Lect. 6. ('If there is no thing to have its essence signified by a definition, then the definition is no different from the explanation of the meaning of a term') I find it interesting that when Wittgenstein asks himself what after all is a *game*? What is it that is common to all games in virtue of which we call them games? his answer has a great deal in common with that of Aristotle and St Thomas when they ask themselves what after all is being? What is it that is common to all beings in virtue of which we say that they are? Wittgenstein points out that there is nothing common. What we have is:

> a complicated network of similarities overlapping and criss-crossing sometimes overall similarities, sometimes similarities of detail.

He compares the concept of game to that of number:

> we extend our concept of number as in spinning a thread we twist fibre on fibre. And the strength of the thread does not reside in the fact that some one thread rims through its whole length, but in the overlapping of many fibres. (*Philosophical Investigations*, 1, 66 and 67.)

Similarly St Thomas points out that there is nothing common to all beings. *Ens non est genus*, and his theory of the general use of the word 'being' is the well-known and often misinterpreted theory of analogy which, however, I cannot discuss at this point.

7. The Aristotelian Alternative – Different Types of Statement

The alternative that the Aristotelian offers to the theory I have discussed above is that 'George is an animal' and 'George is hungry' do not differ in that the former expresses a rule of language while only the latter can be used to make a statement about George, but that both of them can be used to make statements about George; the difference is a difference in the type of statement that they can be used to make. The view that I have been criticizing seems to be that while there may be different types of sentence by which statements may be made about things, there is only one type of statement; and since sentences of the type of 'George is an animal' cannot be used to make this type of statement they cannot be used to make statements at all. The view that I am proposing is that there are different types of statement as well as different types of sentence, that there are in fact at least ten different types of statement. I am further going to suggest that these several types of statement are related to one another in a variety of different ways but that there is no common formula which they all exemplify in virtue of which they are all called statements. This is what I take to be Aristotle's and St Thomas' theory of the Categories or Praedicamenta.

My strongest reason for preferring this theory to that of the Fact/Language-Rule philosophers is that the latter after explaining that sentences like 'George is an animal' merely show the place of 'George' in some language, seem to be left with peculiar insoluble problems about the word 'exists'. They find difficulty in saying what is meant by 'George' being the *name* of something, for they have carefully and accurately demonstrated that the question of whether or not 'George' is the name of anything has nothing to do with its meaning. For example Mr J.L. Evans says with perfect truth:

> The obvious alternative to the Relational Theory of meaning (and one which is gradually supplanting it) is to admit that in considering the question of meaning no reference need be made to any extra-linguistic facts. This must apply to all words, expressions and sentences and no favourites such as logically proper names must be granted exemption. On this theory the meaning of a word is simply the rules which govern its use, and to ask for its meaning is to ask for the rules.[8]

There remains then the question: What are we saying when we say that George exists? When we say this we are certainly not stating an extra-linguistic fact; that George exists cannot be a fact about George; but neither are we giving additional rules for the proper use of 'George' in the English language.

Some people think that any puzzles we have about the word 'exists' are our own fault, because there is no need to have the word in our language. They think that we can get on very well without it and that the puzzles that it generates all arise from the hopeless attempt to treat it as though it had a useful function. In particular they think

---

[8] 'On Meaning and Verification', *Mind* 24, Jan. 1953, p. 9.

that it can never appropriately be used as a predicate attached to a singular subject. I want to show that, on the contrary, this word has a definite part to play in a philosopher's language. More precisely I want to show that we need *some* expression which expresses something about things which is neither a fact about them nor a rule for the linguistic use of their names. I shall show this by an examination of the difference between sentences that do and sentences that do not make statements. This is St Thomas' line of approach to the question of *esse*; for him it is in the *judicium*, the act of stating something truly or falsely, the second operation of the intellect, that we are concerned with *esse*.

> Prima quidem operatio respicit ipsam naturam rei … Secunda vero operatio respicit ipsurn esse rei.[9]

8. Referring and Existence. (a) Subject and Predicate

If we say 'The old man was not a plumber' we have a factual sentence that makes sense, but we cannot claim to be saying something that is true, or even something that is false, unless we are using this sentence to say something about an old man. Simply considered as a sentence it is neither true nor false. It is only when we use it on this or that occasion to talk about this or that old man that we can be right or wrong. To use Mr Strawson's

---

[9]   *In Boet. De Trinitate*. Q. 5, Art 3. (The first operation concerns the very nature of a thing; the second operation concerns the very *esse* of a thing.)

terminology,[10] the sentence becomes a true or false *statement* only when its subject 'The old man' is being used to *refer* to something. The second part of the sentence, the predicate '... was not a plumber,' on the other hand, is not being used to refer, nor is its constituent phrase 'a plumber' being used to refer. We might ask, 'Which old man isn't a plumber?' but it would be stupid to ask, 'Which plumber isn't he?' This doctrine of the different functions of subject and predicate in a statement-making sentence is a favourite one of St Thomas'; he comes back to it again and again, usually in such terms as these:

Terminus in subiecto positus tenetur materialiter, idest pro supposito; positus vero in praedicato tenetur formaliter, idest pro natura significata.[11]

An expression functioning as a subject is taken *materially* to stand for something, but when it functions as predicate it is taken *formally* to signify a nature.

---

10 *Op. cit.*
11 *Summa Theol.* III. 16. 7 ad 4. See also: 1. 13. 12. c; I. 16.2. c; 1. 31. 3 ad 2; 111. 16. 9. c; Ill. 17. 1 ad 3; Met. 9, Lect. 11, n. 1898; 3 Sent. 7. 1. 1. c. This extremely important doctrine has been strangely neglected by Thomists. The only good account of it that I know is an invaluable article by Mr P. Geach, 'Subjects and Predicates', Mind 236, Oct. 1950. Those interested in St Thomas' theory of language will notice that I am taking this distinction (*tenetur materialiter et formaliter*) to be different from the distinction made in e.g. *De Potentia*, 9. 4. c between formal and material *signification*. And, of course, for an expression to be taken materially is not the same as for it to have material *supposition*.

9. (b) Referring and Identity

St Thomas, however, did not think that this was invariably the case. He notes an exception which is of peculiar interest; it is worth turning aside to consider it since it helps to clarify the notion of referring. In the Commentary on the Sentences he notes that in the case of a sentence of the form '*x* is *y*' where '*x*' and '*y*' are both substantives, it may happen that '*y*' is taken *materialiter*, as a referring word, instead of *formaliter*. This case he calls a 'praedicatio per identitatem' as distinct from the common 'praedicatio per informationem' which is more properly a predication.[12] Thus in a predication *per informationem* as, for example, 'George is very stupid,' you are saying that what is referred to by 'George' is very stupid. But in a predication *per identitatem* as, for example, 'George is Mr Smith,' the substantive 'Mr Smith' in the predicate is taken materially in the same way as the subject expression 'George', and so you are saying that what is referred to by 'George' is also referred to by 'Mr Smith'. Thus, for St Thomas, a statement of identity, *unlike* other kinds of statement, asserts that two referring expressions refer to the same thing. This view of identity seems to be the same as that of Wittgenstein in the *Tractatus*:

[12] 3 Sent. 5. Exp. Text. Substantiva (as opposed to adiectiva) significant non tantum formam sed etiam suppositum formae, unde possunt praedicari ratione utriusque; et quando praedicantur ratione suppositi dicitur praedicatio per identitatem, quando autem ratione formae dicitur praedicatio per denominationem sive informationem, et haec est magis proprie praedicatio quia termini in praedicato tenentur formaliter …

'a is identical with b' means that the sign 'a' is replaceable by the sign 'b'.

and

Identity of the object I express by identity of the sign and not by means of the sign of identity. Difference of objects by difference of the signs.[13]

Lord Russell had defined identity as follows:

X and y are identical when every predicative function satisfied by x is also satisfied by y.[14]

In the *Tractatus* Wittgenstein objected:

Russell's definition of '=' won't do, because according to it one cannot say that two objects have all their properties in common. (Even if this proposition is never true it is nevertheless *significant*.)[15]

This view clearly depends on the belief that one can say '*x* is not *y*' significantly as a pure *praedicatio per (non) identitatem* without *eo ipso* attributing any difference of properties to *x* and *y*. It is interesting that Carnap, for example, notices Wittgenstein's objection and brushes it aside:

---

[13] *Tractatus Logico-Philosophicus* (London, 1951), 4.241 and 5.53.
[14] *Principia Mathematica*, p. 168, cf. 13.01.
[15] *Tractatus*, 5.5302.

This objection is dismissed as soon as all properties are understood as including those of position.[16]

It seems clear that, for Carnap, to refer to a thing is the same as to assign to it a certain *position*. For him the properties of what he calls 'position' seem to have a mystical significance akin to that of the primary qualities for Locke. I am not very sure what Carnap does mean by 'position' but I take it that, whatever extensions are made to the ordinary use of the term, only concrete things can have position. One of the important differences between referring to something and assigning a position to it is that we seem to be able to refer by means of abstract nouns as easily as by means of concrete ones. When I say that the prevalence of divorce is a sign of the instability of modern life, I do seem to be referring to either the prevalence of divorce or the instability of modern life, but it is not easy to see how either of these could be assigned a position. It is only by tinkering with the statement in a rather dubious way that one can make it appear equivalent to a statement or set of statements about concrete individuals with positions.[17] As Mr Strawson puts it, the theory of referring 'does not put any limits on the sorts of things that can be referred to. It puts

---

[16] *Logical Syntax of Language*, p. 50.
[17] I do not mean to suggest that there could be a statement about divorce unless there were individuals who were divorced. For we can only make statements about what exists, and divorce cannot exist except as the divorce of some people. Nevertheless the statement is about the divorce and not about the people, and it is the divorce that is referred to. St Thomas makes this point very clearly against Avicenna, *Comm. in Met.*, V, Lect. 9, n. 894.

no premium on concreteness.'[18] In fact referring cannot be the same as assigning a position even though pointing in a certain direction is a common way of referring to individuals, for in assigning a position we are either simply adding further predicates to the subject or else we are stating that what is named by the subject has a certain position. In the former case our sentence is no more a statement than it was before the additional predicates were added – we still need to presuppose that the subject refers – in the latter case we have included the presupposition of reference in the statement of position. Thus the sentence 'The whale is travelling rather fast' does not become a statement simply because it is expanded to 'That whale over there beside the lighthouse, near the seagull, is travelling rather fast.' Both of these are simply sentences and only become statements when it is presupposed that their subjects refer to something. It is very important to see that the referring character of the subject is not part of what is asserted by a statement When I assert that George is hungry I am not asserting that 'George' has reference, I am presupposing it, because unless I am presupposing it I will not have said anything true or false; I will merely have enunciated a sentence.

10. The Presuppositions of Existence and of Definition

For convenience I am going to use the word 'real' in the following sense: When an expression 'S' that functions as subject in a sentence has reference I am going to say that S is real. This is merely a device for avoiding circumlocutions.

---

[18] *Introduction to Logical Theory*, p. 145.

171

(I am going to suggest later that 'S is real' is *not* used in the same way as 'S exists' for if the latter is to be used in a technical Aristotelian sense the two will only be the same for certain kinds of substitution for 'S'.) When I assert that George is hungry, I presuppose, but do not (in the ordinary sense of the word) *imply* that George is real. If I said, 'George is hungry so he must be real,' I would not be making use of the sort of implication that I would be using if I said 'George is free, white and twenty-one so he must be white.' I have used this example before in a different context; part of the Aristotelian theory of statements is that these two contexts are not so very different. I said before (Sect. 5) that the assertion that *George is an animal* is presupposed by but not part of what is asserted by the assertion that George is hungry. I am now saying that the assertion that *George is real* is presupposed by but not part of what is asserted by the assertion that *George is hungry*. Let us, for the moment, call sentences like 'George is an animal' definitional sentences, and sentences like 'George is real' referential sentences. The central doctrine of the Aristotelian theory is that in the case of certain subject expressions (of which, as it happens, 'George' is not one) what is asserted by means of the referential sentence is the same as what is asserted by means of the definitional sentence. Such subject expressions are the proper subjects of the predicate '... exists'; they are, in St Thomas' language, names of *entia per se*, and *entia per se* are either substances or qualities or quantities, etc. All other subject expressions are the names of *entia per accidens*; of this we shall see much more later.

The classical example of a subject expression of this special kind is 'The human being'. According to the Aristotelian what is asserted by saying 'The human being is real' (or, by saying '"The human being" has reference') is the same as what is asserted by saying 'The human being is a rational animal,' and hence by the rule just given 'The human being is real' is the same as 'The human being exists.' Thus just as when the factual sentence 'The human being is white' is used to make a statement, we assert concerning the human being that he is white; so when the definitional sentence 'The human being is a rational animal' is used to make a statement, we assert concerning the human being that it exists and nothing more. Of course it is by no means necessary that a definitional sentence should be used to make a statement; no sentence is, as such, a statement. When it is not used to make a statement it is neither true nor false but merely expresses a rule of language that has been decided upon. But if we do ask, 'Is it *true* that a human being is a rational animal?' we can only be asking if there is a human being, just as if we ask, 'Is it *true* that a knight moves like this?' we can only be asking if there are games of chess. The difference between a definitional sentence used as a rule of language and used as a statement of existence, is not that any reference is made to any extra-linguistic *fact*, for the existence of a cow is not a fact about the cow nor a fact about anything else, unless it is a fact about some unintelligible metaphysical entity called 'The World' or 'Reality' or whatever.

The difference between such rather special subject expressions as 'The human being' and the vast majority of subject expressions in the English language is that when we construct a sentence which can be used to express the rules of language for 'The human being' we can also use this sentence as a statement to assert that the human being exists and nothing more, whereas with nearly all other subject expressions this is not so. To know that something is a human being is purely and simply to know *what* it is, but to know, for example, that something is a postman is not simply to know *what* it is, but also to know some facts about it, that it is employed to deliver letters, etc. Thus the sentence giving the rules for the use of 'The postman' is (let us say) 'The postman is the human being that delivers letters.' But if we use this sentence as a statement we do not merely state the existence of something but also the extra-linguistic *fact* that it delivers letters. The postman could continue to exist if this became no longer a fact, if he retired or got another job, but he could not continue to exist if he ceased to be a human being. To say that he is a human being is to give, so to say, the minimum determination that he must have in order to be at all.

If I say 'The postman is insane' you might answer, 'Yes, that's true, though as a matter of fact he isn't the postman really, he's my uncle wearing the postman's uniform.' But you could not sensibly reply: 'Yes, that's true, though as a matter of fact it isn't the postman really, it's a statue dressed up in the postman's uniform' because it does not make sense to say that a statue is or is not insane. Still less could you sensibly reply: 'Well that's only partly true because it isn't really the postman at all; I don't know what it is but it's some x' for you have absolutely no notion whether '*x*' is a subject to which '… is insane' can be appropriately attached. Nevertheless there have been logicians who have cheerfully offered, 'There is an *x* such that *x* is a postman and *x* is insane' as an equivalent of 'A postman is insane.' According to the Aristotelian, the least that is required in order that 'A postman is insane' should be a statement (i.e. both a sentence that makes sense and one the subject of which has reference) is that 'A postman' should refer to something of which it makes sense to say that it is insane or not insane, but there is no need that it should refer to something that is a postman. Thus the Aristotelian would say that 'A postman is insane' might be rewritten as 'A human being (who delivers letters) is insane.' The clause in brackets represents a factual presupposition incorporated into the subject expression which may turn out to be mistaken without damaging the original statement unduly. But if you say, 'An *x* (who is a human being who delivers letters) is insane,' the clause in brackets is absolutely essential to understanding the sentence, for without knowing that *x* is a human being you could not know that it made sense to say that *x* is insane. '*X*' is a variable and a variable is not a very, very general name; it is a labelled blank space. As Aristotle and St Thomas point out at laborious length, the condition for '— is walking and — is white' to make a statement is not merely that some subject expressions should be put in the two spaces, nor in order to assert that the walking thing is white is it sufficient to note that the *same* subject expression should be put in the two spaces; we must put in a subject expression of a definite meaning, a subject expression to which both '… is walking' and '… is white' are appropriate. 'The walking (thing)', as Aristotle puts it, 'walks and is white in virtue of something else besides'. Before anything can walk or be white or both, it must be something of a definite kind (the kind of thing that can walk or be white); and to say that this is *what it is* is to make the same assertion as we make when we say that it exists.

11. *Entia per accidens* and *Entia per se*. (a) *Entia per accidens* as Logical Constructions

The distinction between subjects such as 'The human being' and subjects such as 'The postman' is the distinction I mentioned before (Sect. 4) between subjects the meaning of which exerts only one kind of restriction over the predicates that can be attached to them to yield factual sentences that make sense, and those the meaning of which exerts two kinds of restriction. It is the distinction between meanings that are given by simple rules and those that are given by rules with particular exceptions. 'The postman is an exact multiple of three' is excluded by the first kind of restriction (which also excludes 'The postman is *not* an exact multiple of three') whereas 'The postman is not employed to deliver letters' is excluded by the second (which does not exclude 'The postman *is* employed to deliver letters'). Expressions like 'The human being' only exercise the first sort of restriction. St Thomas' way of distinguishing the two kinds of subject is to say that a postman is an *ens per accidens* whereas a human being is an *ens per se*.

176

Scholastic philosophers who have some familiarity with St Thomas' terminology should beware of the temptation to confuse *ens per accidens* with *ens accidentale*. The distinction between *ens per se* and *ens per accidens* is not the distinction between substance and accident; accidents are *entia per se* just as truly as substances are. St Thomas is very insistent that the categories are a classification of *entia per se*. The difference between substance and accident is not that only substances are properly said to exist (*ens per se*) while accidents are only said to exist *per accidens*, but that while both are properly said to exist, the predicate '... exists' is used analogically of them; it is said *per prius* of substances and *per posterius* of accidents. This point can be put by saying that whereas all statement-making sentences whose subjects are names of *entia per accidens* can be shown to be equivalent to statement-making sentences whose subjects are names of *entia per se*, it is not true that statements about accidents can be thus reduced to statements about substances. Nothing but sheer ignorance could lead to the belief that St Thomas' theory of substance is the theory that all statements are analysable into statements about substances, or the even more fantastic belief that St Thomas, noticing that a lot of Latin sentences contained a subject and a predicate, thought that the subject ought to stand for a substance and the predicate for a quantity, quality, relation, etc.[19]

---

[19] To see the absurdity of this it is sufficient to read a passage (e.g. 1 Sent. 22. 1. 1 ad 3) where St Thomas carefully distinguishes the grammarian's use of 'substantia' in e.g. 'nomen Significat substantia cum qualitate' from the logician's use when *substantia is* the name of one of the ten categories.

One way of putting St Thomas' theory would be to say that an *ens per accidens* is a logical construction out of *entia per se*.[20] Thus, Mr A.J. Ayer once wrote:

> The assertion that tables are logical constructions out of sense contents ... is tantamount to saying that sentences which contain the symbol 'table' ... can all be translated into sentences of the same language which do not contain that symbol, not any of its synonyms, but do contain certain symbols that stand for sense contents.[21]

If for 'Sense contents' you substitute '*entia per se*', and if you give a charitable interpretation to 'stands for', you get a fair account of St Thomas' theory of *entia per accidens*. Thus 'A postman was insane' can be translated to 'A human being was employed to deliver letters and he was insane.' This kind of translation can be carried further since both insanity and being employed to deliver letters are still *entia per accidens*, and an empirical investigation of the ways in which we use 'insane' and 'employed to deliver letters' will enable us to expand the sentence into one containing only expressions that stand for the *entia per se* of which these are logical constructions. To make such a translation is not, of course, to produce a preferable way of saying that the postman was insane; it will be cumbersome, stilted and less readily intelligible; its only advantage will be that it exhibits unambiguously the way in which it makes sense.

---

[20] I owe this suggestion, like so much else in this article, to Fr Columba Ryan, OP.

[21] *Language Truth and Logic* (London, 1949), pp. 63–64.

12. (b) *Entia per accidens* are described; *entia per se* are defined

It is impossible in a short article to enter into the complications which arise from the circumstance that in any language actually in use there are practically no words for *entia per se*. This is simply because, as St Thomas repeatedly points out, we name things according to their outstanding characteristics, according to the properties that interest us and which we find useful for recognising things in the ordinary course of events. For practical purposes we are not usually interested in what things are but only in how they affect us or how we may use them. Generally speaking our names are abbreviated descriptions rather than abbreviated definitions. A description of a horse tells us what we may expect to find when we examine a horse; a definition merely tells us what the horse must be in order to be at all. It tells us what it would make sense to say that we have found or not found. The same definition is compatible with two descriptions which differ on every point, it is only incompatible with two descriptions which have not got the same points.

The descriptional character of our names gives them a certain looseness of application that Professor Waismann has called 'open texture'.[22] We can never, as Locke saw, come to the end of describing a material object; there is always something further that might be said. A descriptional name never completely circumscribes the thing

---

[22] '*Verifiability*'. In the collection *Logic and Language*, ed. Antony Flew (Oxford, 1952), p. 117.

named; we are perpetually confronted by the possibility of the thing developing a new property. Must we then find a new word for it? or must we expand the sense of the old word? The answers to these questions are, of course, largely a matter of linguistic convenience. The so-called theory of Substance which seeks to regulate the answer by finding a stable core of essential characteristics which may not be changed without changing the name, surrounded by a penumbra of less essential characteristics which can be dispensed with, should be sufficiently discredited by now. The interesting thing however is that the question necessarily arises. It is in principle impossible to construct descriptional names which correspond to things: there must be constant shifts of meaning and adjustments in order to maintain a working approxi-mation. There is nothing regrettable about this; it just happens to be how every practicable language works. The reason for it is that no description or enumeration of characteristics expresses what it is for a thing to be; things do not come into being in virtue of having this or that characteristic nor cease to be in virtue of losing it. Things are not facts nor collections of facts, they are the topics of a certain range of facts. To say that a factual sentence makes a true statement is not the same as saying that what is named by the subject exists, for what is named by the subject would be real (or – if it is an *ens per se* – would exist) if the statement were false. What exists is a topic of disagreement. A description gives you one side of the possible disagreement – the majority opinion; a definition simply tells you what the disagreement is about.

Thus it is in the definition that St Thomas finds the point of contact between language and things; definitions are incorrigible: they are not adjusted to meet new facts because they do not assert or deny facts; they are merely rejected if we are compelled to state new facts outside their range. From the point of view of language the *definition* founds a language game; these and these things may be asserted or denied. From the point of view of things the *essence*, what the thing is, founds an object of experience; these and these things may or may not be the case. No accumulation of facts about a thing is equivalent to what the thing is, just as no accumulation of sensible sentences whose subject is 'S' is equivalent to the meaning of 'S'.

Notice that if my interpretation of him is correct it is through the search for the definition, the linguistic expression of *ens* that St Thomas approaches the question of *esse*, or the proper use of '… exists', and not *vice versa*. It does not seem to be his view that we all start off by knowing what 'exists' means in virtue of our empirical experience, the experience, as people say, of the concrete existential chair. Whether or not I am here differing from those contemporary Thomists who like to speak of the 'existentialism of St Thomas' I do not know, for I am never certain of what exactly they mean by this.

13. Types of *entia per se* – the Categories

In a certain sense it is misleading to say that St Thomas has a theory of substance. He has a theory of *Praedicamenta* or Categories only one of which is the category of substance. The ten categories represent a classification of definables, or *entia per se*, according to the ways in which they exist; or, what is the same thing, it is a classification of statements according to the ways in which they are statements.[23] It is clear that there are different kinds of statement since the statement which results from predicating the definition (or part of the definition) of something, which simply asserts the existence of what I have called a 'topic of disagreement', is irreducibly different from any statement or statements made by factual sentences on one or other side of the disagreement. When I say that a man is a rational animal (a statement in the category of substance) I merely assert his existence, or announce that a certain range of factual sentences will be statement-making sentences; when I assert that he is pink I state a fact about him but I do not by that statement announce his existence. It is true that the factual statement (which is in the category of quality) does presuppose – in a special sense of presuppose – the statement in the category of substance, but this is not part of what it asserts. Thus (supposing for present purposes that being pink, or pinkness, unlike e.g. being a trump or a centre-forward, were an *ens per se*) to attribute pinkness to something is to make a statement in a different sense of 'statement' from making a statement by attributing humanity or rational-animality to something. This is what is meant by saying that pinkness belongs to one category

---

[23] *Comm. in Met.* V, Lect. 9, n. 890. 'Oportet quod ens contrahatur ad diversa genera secundum diversum modum praedicandi qui consequitur diversum modum essendi ... et propter hoc ea in quae dividitur ens primo dicuntur "praedicamenta" quia distinguuntur secundum diversum modum praedicandi.'

(quality) and humanity to another (substance); pinkness exists in one way and humanity in another.

Some people would be doubtful of the propriety of saying that pinkness exists at all, on the grounds that it is an abstraction whereas only concrete things exist; but in this they are, I think, the victims of a muddle. Properly speaking, 'concrete' and 'abstract' are grammarian's adjectives qualifying nouns and not things; things are neither concrete nor abstract. In St Thomas' terminology the difference between concreteness and abstractness is not one of 'res significata' but of 'modus significandi'. The peculiarity of a quality, such as pinkness, is not that it exists, or subsists, or fails to exist, *abstractly*, but that 'pinkness' can only refer to an existent quality which is the pinkness of some substance, for there cannot *be* pinkness which is not something's pinkness. This is what is meant by saying that pinkness can only exist in a substance. This is not like saying that fish can only exist in the water, for the whole of what it is to be pinkness is the being pink of something: an accident is a being 'cuius esse est inesse'.

14. Transcendental Words.

Thus, in distinguishing the categories St Thomas is distinguishing ten ways of existing or ten senses of the word 'exists', and correspondingly, ten senses of the words 'true' and 'statement' and hence of 'thing', 'something', 'topic of disagreement', etc. A great deal of his metaphysical writing is concerned with an analysis of the behaviour of words of this kind which he calls 'transcendental words' because they transcend the categories and belong to them all. To say that something is white or four feet tall or upside down is to attribute something to it in one or other of the accidental categories: to say that it is a human being is to state something about it in the category of substance; to say that it is a quality or a relation or a place or a time is also to make a statement about it in the category of substance ('Whiteness is a quality' makes a statement in the category of substance, for it says – partially – *what* whiteness is), but to say of it that it exists or is *something* or that there are *statements* about it which are true or false is not to make a statement in any determinate category. We cannot assign any simple meaning to transcendental words because this would be to restrict their application to a particular category; in fact their meanings change according to the category in which they are applied. In the metaphysics of St Thomas there are no such questions as 'What is existence?' or 'What is truth?' or 'What are statements ultimately about?' We can, of course, explain the meaning of one transcendental word in terms of others; we can say, for instance, that a statement is true when it states what is so; but 'is so' suffers the same shifts in meaning as do 'statement' and 'true'. This means that there can be no rules for the translation of all statements into a single universal language about a single reality called 'the world', that there can be no all-comprehensive Principle of Verification, but only many principles according to the many senses of 'verification'. There is no one kind of reality that we 'ought' to talk about, but many which are real in different senses.

15. The Theory of Analogy

Once we have eliminated the metaphysical pipe-dream of discovering the Nature of Truth, etc., we can begin to enquire how it is that we do use the same transcendental words in different contexts although their meaning changes from one context to another. It is in answer to this that St Thomas first develops his theory of analogy. I have, of course, no intention of dealing with this theory here but it may be useful to notice its beginnings in the theory of categories. St Thomas asks how it is that the same predicate can be used in all ten categories and he notes that although there can be no form, or way of being, common to things in any two categories (since the categories are precisely different ways of being) the nine accidental categories have at least, and at most, this in common that they are all dependent (each in its own way in nine different senses of 'dependent') on substance. No statement in a category of accident can be true (or false) unless a statement in the category of substance is true; or, to put it in terms of another transcendental, a quantity cannot *be* which is not the quantity of some substance, and a quality cannot *be* which is not the quality of some substance. This is what he means by saying that 'exists' (and the rest of the transcendental words) are used *per prius* of substance and *per posterius* of accidents because of their dependence on substance. It means one thing for a quality to exist and another thing for a quantity to exist, but each use of 'exist' is related in some way to the use of 'exist' in which we speak of a substance existing. St Thomas illustrates this by comparison with the fairly common linguistic phenomenon of the transferred

185

epithet. We speak of a healthy man as having a healthy complexion and living on good healthy food, and in such cases the adjective 'healthy' is used *per prius* of the man and *per posterius* of the complexion and the food. There is nothing common to the complexion and the food in virtue of which we call them both healthy, except that in each case the healthiness depends in some way on the healthiness of the man; healthy food is the sort of food that makes men healthy, a healthy complexion is the sort of complexion that healthy men have. In the same way there is nothing in common between a quality and a relation in virtue of which we say that they both exist except that in each case the existence depends in some way on the existence of a substance. There is of course much more to be said about the theory of analogy and the peculiar behaviour of transcendental words; I have only said this much here in order to make a transition between the discussion of St Thomas' general view of language and things which I have attempted here and the special question of the use of language about God.

186

APPENDIX 2

Editions of St Thomas's Writings Cited in this Volume

Summa Theologiae, ed. P. Caramello (Marietti: Turin/Rome, 1950).

Summa Contra Gentiles, editio leonina manualis (Comissio Leonina: Rome, 1934).

Scriptum Supra Libros Sententiarum, vols 1, 2 and 3, ed. P. Mandonnet (Lethielleux: Paris, 1929).

Quaestiones Disputatae De Potentia Dei, vol. 1, in *Quaestiones Disputatae et Quaestiones Duodecim Quodlibetales*, 5 vols (Marietti: Turin/Rome, 1942).

Quaestiones Disputatae De Malo, vol. 2 (Marietti: Turin/Rome, 1942).

Quaestiones Disputatae De Veritate, vols 3–4 (Marietti: Turin/Rome, 1942).

Quaestiones Quodlibetales, vol. 5 (Marietti: Turin/Rome, 1942)

Expositio Super Librum Boethii De Trinitate, ed. B. Decker (Brill: Leiden, 1955).

In Decem Libros Ethicorum Aristotelis ad Nichomachum Expositio, ed. A.M. Pirotta (Marietti: Turin/Rome, 1934).

In Metaphysicam Aristotelis Commentaria, ed. M.R. Cathala (Marietti: Turin/Rome, 1935).

In Octo Libros Physicorum Aristotelis Expositio, ed. P. M. Maggiolo (Marietti: Turin/Rome, 1954).

In Libros Aristotelis De Caelo et Mundo Expositio, ed. R.M. Spiazzi (Marietti: Turin/Rome, 1952).

In Librum Primum Aristotelis De Generatione et Corruptione, ed. R.M. Spiazzi (Marietti: Turin/Rome, 1952).

In Aristotelis Librum De Anima Commentarium, ed. A.M. Pirotta (Marietti: Turin/Rome, 1936).

In Librum de Sensu et Sensato Commentarium, ed.
R.M. Spiazzi (Marietti: Turin/Rome, 1949).

In Librum de Memoria et Reminiscentia Commentarium, ed. R.M. Spiazzi (Marietti: Turin/Rome, 1949).

In Aristotelis Libros Peri Hermeneias et Posteriorum Analyticorum Expositio, ed. R.M. Spiazzi (Marietti: Turin/Rome, 1955).

De Ente et Essentia. In *Opuscula Philosophica*, ed.
R.M. Spiazzi (Marietti: Turin/Rome, 1954).

De Principiis Naturae ad Fratrem Sylvestrum (Marietti: Turin/Rome, 1954).

BIBLIOGRAPHY

Adams, Marilyn McCord and Adams, Robert
    Merrihew (eds), *The Problem of Evil* (Oxford
    University Press: Oxford, 1990).

Aertsen, Jan, *Nature and Creature: Thomas Aquinas's
    Way of Thought* (E.J. Brill: Leiden, 1988).

Ahern, M.B., *The Problem of Evil* (Routledge &
    Kegan Paul: London, 1971).

Anscombe, G.E.M. and Geach, P.T., *Three
    Philosophers* (Basil Blackwell: Oxford, 1961).

Chenu, M.-D., *Towards Understanding Saint Thomas*
    (Henry Regnery Co.: Chicago, IL, 1964).

Davies, Brian, *The Reality of God and the Problem of
    Evil* (Continuum: London and New York,
    2006).

Geach, P.T., 'Good and Evil', *Analysis* 17 (1956).

Howard-Snyder, Daniel (ed.), *The Evidential
    Argument from Evil* (Indiana University Press:
    Bloomington, IN and Indianapolis, 1996).

Martin, C.F.J., *Thomas Aquinas: God and
    Explanation* (Edinburgh University Press:
    Edinburgh, 1997).

Pieper, Josef, *The Silence of Saint Thomas* (Henry
    Regnery Co.: Chicago, IL, 1965).

Ross, James F., 'Creation II', in Alfred J. Freddoso
    (ed.), *The Existence and Nature of God*
    (University of Notre Dame Press: Notre Dame,
    IN and London, 1983).

White, Victor, *God the Unknown and Other Essays*
    (The Harvill Press: London, 1956).

Wippel, John F., *Metaphysical Themes in Thomas
    Aquinas* (The Catholic University of America
    Press: Washington, DC, 1984).

Wippel, John F., *The Metaphysical Thought of Thomas Aquinas* (The Catholic University of America Press: Washington, DC, 2000.

INDEX